The New York Times

IN THE HEADLINES

Deportation

WHO GOES AND WHO STAYS?

THE NEW YORK TIMES EDITORIAL STAFF

Published in 2019 by The New York Times® Educational Publishing
in association with The Rosen Publishing Group, Inc.
29 East 21st Street, New York, NY 10010

First Edition

The New York Times
Alex Ward: Editorial Director, Book Development
Phyllis Collazo: Photo Rights/Permissions Editor
Heidi Giovine: Administrative Manager

Rosen Publishing
Megan Kellerman: Managing Editor
Marcia Amidon Lusted: Editor
Greg Tucker: Creative Director
Brian Garvey: Art Director

Cataloging-in-Publication Data
Names: New York Times Company.
Title: Deportation: who goes and who stays? / edited by the New
York Times editorial staff.
Description: New York : New York Times Educational Publishing,
2019. | Series: In the headlines | Includes glossary and index.
Identifiers: ISBN 9781642821123 (library bound) | ISBN
9781642821116 (pbk.) | ISBN 9781642821130 (ebook)
Subjects: LCSH: Illegal aliens—Government policy—United
States—Juvenile literature. | Deportation—United States—
Juvenile literature. | Immigration enforcement—United
States—Juvenile literature. | United States—Emigration and
immigration—Government policy—Juvenile literature.
Classification: LCC JV6483.D476 2019 | DDC 364.6'8—dc23

Manufactured in the United States of America

On the cover: Immigration officials make an arrest in April 2010
at a shuttle business in Tucson, Ariz. believed to be part of a
smuggling ring; Monica Almeida/The New York Times.

Contents

CHAPTER 3

Debating Who Should Stay and the Dreamers

CHAPTER 4

Families at the Border

CHAPTER 5

Global Impact

Introduction

IMMIGRATION HAS BEEN a reoccurring and often controversial issue since before the founding of the United States as a country. While the United States has long cherished its representation as a "melting pot," a place where many nationalities, races and cultures have come together and blended into a strong, new whole, the reality is that immigration has often created strong feelings as to who should be considered a "real" American and who should not. Even the language used to convey the status of someone who is not American-born is derogatory: They are called "resident aliens" or "illegal aliens," even in government literature. It almost seems a contradiction that the Statue of Liberty, one of the first sites that once welcomed immigrants to the United States, has a plaque on its base with the sonnet "New Colossus" by Emma Lazarus, which includes the line, "Give me your tired, your poor, your huddled masses yearning to breathe free."

The reality of what immigrants encounter when entering the United States is rarely welcoming. Throughout history, immigrants have experienced varying degrees of official scrutiny in order to move to the United States and become residents. Their numbers were extremely high, especially as a result of events such as world wars, the Holocaust, the Irish potato famine and other catastrophic political, religious and natural disasters that forced people to flee intolerable living conditions.

Between 1892 and 1954, when Ellis Island in New York City was the busiest station in the country for arriving immigrants, 12 million people were processed there alone. Those who succeeded in gaining entry often faced a new round of discrimination from established Americans. Ethnic groups such as the Irish were characterized as lazy, unintelligent, criminal and alcoholic, and were often discriminated against in hiring by the words "No Irish Need Apply." They resorted to jobs such as digging ditches, laying rail lines, cleaning houses and working in mills, all for low pay. Working-class Americans feared that Irish immigrants were taking jobs away from them. Even their religion, Catholicism, put them at odds with American Protestants. Ultimately, people who shared anti-Catholic and anti-immigration sentiments formed the American Party, whose members vowed only to elect native-born citizens to office. Their slogans included "Americans must rule America!"

Oddly, these 19th-century immigration issues have never really gone away, and the question of who should be allowed to stay in the United States and who should be forced to leave has always simmered below the surface. Racism, religious intolerance and other factors have contributed to anti-immigration sentiments and have been widely debated. During the 2016 presidential campaign, candidate Donald Trump won many followers with his stance on immigration: mainly that immigrants (especially those who were in the country illegally) were taking jobs away from Americans, clogging the social welfare system, and generating much of the crime in the United States.

One of Trump's first actions after his inauguration as president was to issue a series of executive orders banning the admission of anyone from seven primarily Muslim countries into the United States, as well as any refugees from Syria, and granting immigration priority to Christians over Muslims. This action created chaos in the nation's major international airports, as people flying into the United States, some with legitimate visas, were refused entry. The travel ban initiated by Trump was temporarily rescinded, but was upheld by the Supreme Court in June 2018.

President Trump, a vocal opponent of many forms of immigration, said in May 2018: "[The United States has] the dumbest laws on immigration in the world. We have people coming into the country or trying to come in — we're stopping a lot of them. You wouldn't believe how

President Donald Trump signs an executive order on immigration at the Pentagon in Arlington, Va., on Jan. 27, 2017. For the president, the chaos of the travel ban and the subsequent legal challenges were the first, sharp evidence that he could exert power over a federal bureaucracy he had criticized on the campaign trail.

bad these people are. These aren't people, these are animals, and we're taking them out of the country at a level and a rate that's never happened before."

The question of immigration, and especially who should be allowed to come to the United States, who should remain here, and who should be deported and sent back to their countries of origin is a controversial and divisive issue. People are intensely divided as to how they feel, sometimes to the point of violence. There are far-reaching implications to welcoming or barring people from the country who might actually bring their own wealth of knowledge and ability to contribute to the United States. It is not an issue that can be easily resolved or even easily discussed.

CHAPTER 1

Immigration Controversy

Since the election of President Donald Trump in 2016, controversy and fear surrounding immigration to the United States has grown intensely. While some feel immigrants should be able to start new lives here and that they make meaningful contributions to American society, others feel immigrants, especially illegal ones, take jobs away from Americans, as well as receive health care and other social welfare benefits. The discussion divides the country every day, and confusion surrounding the Trump administration's immigration policy has further complicated the issue.

Trump Supports Plan to Cut Legal Immigration by Half

BY PETER BAKER | AUG. 2, 2017

WASHINGTON — President Trump embraced a proposal on Wednesday to slash legal immigration to the United States in half within a decade by sharply curtailing the ability of American citizens and legal residents to bring family members into the country.

The plan would enact the most far-reaching changes to the system of legal immigration in decades and represents the president's latest effort to stem the flow of newcomers to the United States. Since taking office, he has barred many visitors from select Muslim-majority countries, limited the influx of refugees, increased immigration arrests and pressed to build a wall along the southern border.

In asking Congress to curb legal immigration, Mr. Trump intensified a debate about national identity, economic growth, worker fairness and American values that animated his campaign last year. Critics said the proposal would undercut the fundamental vision of the United States as a haven for the poor and huddled masses, while the president and his allies said the country had taken in too many low-skilled immigrants for too long to the detriment of American workers.

"This legislation will not only restore our competitive edge in the 21st century, but it will restore the sacred bonds of trust between America and its citizens," Mr. Trump said at a White House event alongside two Republican senators sponsoring the bill. "This legislation demonstrates our compassion for struggling American families who deserve an immigration system that puts their needs first and that puts America first."

In throwing his weight behind a bill, Mr. Trump added one more long-odds priority to a legislative agenda already packed with them in the wake of the defeat of legislation to repeal and replace President Barack Obama's health care program. The president has already vowed to overhaul the tax code and rebuild the nation's roads, airports and other infrastructure.

But by endorsing legal immigration cuts, a move he has long supported, Mr. Trump returned to a theme that has defined his short political career and excites his conservative base at a time when his poll numbers continue to sink. Just 33 percent of Americans approved of his performance in the latest Quinnipiac University survey, the lowest rating of his presidency, and down from 40 percent a month ago.

Democrats and some Republicans quickly criticized the move. "Instead of catching criminals, Trump wants to tear apart communities and punish immigrant families that are making valuable contributions to our economy," said Tom Perez, the chairman of the Democratic National Committee. "That's not what America stands for."

The bill, sponsored by Senators Tom Cotton of Arkansas and David Perdue of Georgia, would institute a merit-based system to determine who is admitted to the country and granted legal residency green cards, favoring applicants based on skills, education and language ability rather than relations with people already here. The proposal revives an idea included in broader immigration legislation supported by President George W. Bush that died in 2007.

More than one million people are granted legal residency each year, and the proposal would reduce that by 41 percent in its first year and 50 percent by its 10th year, according to projections cited by its sponsors. The reductions would come largely from those brought in through family connections. The number of immigrants granted legal residency on the basis of job skills, about 140,000, would remain roughly the same.

Under the current system, most legal immigrants are admitted to the United States based on family ties. American citizens can sponsor spouses, parents and minor children for an unrestricted number of visas, while siblings and adult children are given preferences for a limited number of visas available to them. Legal permanent residents holding green cards can also sponsor spouses and children.

In 2014, 64 percent of immigrants admitted with legal residency were immediate relatives of American citizens or sponsored by family members. Just 15 percent entered through employment-based preferences, according to the Migration Policy Institute, an independent research organization. But that does not mean that those who came in on family ties were necessarily low skilled or uneducated. The legislation would award points based on education, ability to speak English, high-paying job offers, age, record of achievement and entrepreneurial initiative. But while it would still allow spouses and minor children of Americans and legal residents to come in, it would eliminate preferences for other relatives, like siblings and adult children. The bill would create a renewable temporary visa for older-adult parents who come for caretaking purposes.

The legislation would limit refugees offered permanent residency to 50,000 a year and eliminate a diversity visa lottery that the sponsors said does not promote diversity. The senators said their bill was meant to emulate systems in Canada and Australia.

The projections cited by the sponsors said legal immigration would decrease to 637,960 after a year and to 539,958 after a decade. "Our current system does not work," Mr. Perdue said. "It keeps America from being competitive and it does not meet the needs of our economy today."

Mr. Cotton said low-skilled immigrants pushed down wages for those who worked with their hands. "For some people, they may think that that's a symbol of America's virtue and generosity," he said. "I think it's a symbol that we're not committed to working-class Americans, and we need to change that."

But Senator Lindsey Graham, Republican of South Carolina, noted that agriculture and tourism were his state's top two industries. "If this proposal were to become law, it would be devastating to our state's economy, which relies on this immigrant work force," he said. "Hotels, restaurants, golf courses and farmers," he added, "will tell you this proposal to cut legal immigration in half would put their business in peril."

Cutting legal immigration would make it harder for Mr. Trump to reach the stronger economic growth that he has promised. Bringing in more workers, especially during a time of low unemployment, increases the size of an economy. Critics said the plan would result in labor shortages, especially in lower-wage jobs that many Americans do not want.

The National Immigration Forum, an advocacy group, said the country was already facing a work force gap of 7.5 million jobs by 2020. "Cutting legal immigration for the sake of cutting immigration would cause irreparable harm to the American worker and their family," said Ali Noorani, the group's executive director.

Surveys show most Americans believe legal immigration benefits the country. In a Gallup poll in January, 41 percent of Americans were satisfied with the overall level of immigration, 11 percentage points higher than the year before and the highest since the question was first asked in 2001. Still, 53 percent of Americans remained dissatisfied.

The plan endorsed by Mr. Trump generated a fiery exchange at the White House briefing when Stephen Miller, the president's policy adviser and a longtime advocate of immigration limits, defended the proposal. Pressed for statistics to back up claims that immigration was costing Americans jobs, he cited several studies that have been debated by experts.

"But let's also use common sense here, folks," Mr. Miller said. "At the end of the day, why do special interests want to bring in more low-skill workers?"

He rejected the argument that immigration policy should also be based on compassion. "Maybe it's time we had compassion for American workers," he said. When a reporter read him some of the words from the Statue of Liberty — "Give me your tired, your poor, your huddled masses yearning to breathe free" — Mr. Miller dismissed them. "The poem that you're referring to was added later," he said. "It's not actually part of the original Statue of Liberty."

He noted that in 1970, the United States allowed in only a third as many legal immigrants as it now does: "Was that violating or not violating the Statue of Liberty law of the land?"

White House Pressed Unsuccessfully to End Immigration Program

BY RON NIXON AND EILEEN SULLIVAN | NOV. 9, 2017

WASHINGTON — The White House unsuccessfully tried to pressure the Homeland Security Department to end a program that allows hundreds of thousands of people from countries affected by natural disasters or violence to live in the United States without fear of being deported, according to people familiar with the discussions.

John F. Kelly, the White House chief of staff, made an 11th-hour plea to Elaine Duke, the acting Homeland Security secretary, ahead of a deadline this past Monday to decide about the status of immigrants in the program from Honduras and Nicaragua.

Ms. Duke ultimately delayed for six months a decision on the status of immigrants from Honduras, saying she had concluded after an internal department review that she did not have enough information about conditions in the country to decide. But she ended the protected status for thousands of immigrants from Nicaragua who came to the United States illegally after Hurricane Mitch in 1998.

Accounts of her phone calls with Mr. Kelly laid bare the strains between Trump administration officials trying to reduce both legal and illegal immigration — a campaign promise of President Trump's — and career immigration officials who see those efforts as overly broad and harsh.

The internal tensions over the administration's immigration agenda were on display in discrepancies among descriptions of the calls.

A White House official said that Mr. Kelly had encouraged Ms. Duke to make a decision but did not pressure her to end the program.

But two other people briefed on the exchange said Ms. Duke had informed the White House over the weekend of her decision to postpone ending the program for Hondurans. Soon afterward, the two people said, Mr. Kelly called Ms. Duke from Asia, where he was traveling with Mr. Trump, to tell her she had made the wrong decision and to reconsider.

Mr. Kelly's message to Ms. Duke was that she needed to reverse course and end the program immediately, according to one of the people briefed on the call, who, like the others, asked for anonymity to describe a private discussion.

Mr. Kelly raised none of the issues about conditions in Honduras, the person said. Mr. Kelly's focus was on a smooth confirmation process for Mr. Trump's pick to run the department, Kirstjen M. Nielsen, and avoiding any steps that would jeopardize the administration's immigration policies.

A Homeland Security spokesman denied that account.

"It is perfectly normal for members of the White House team to weigh in on major decisions," Tyler Q. Houlton, the spokesman, said on Thursday.

And the White House official said that neither Ms. Nielsen's name nor the subject of her confirmation hearing came up during Mr. Kelly's call with Ms. Duke.

Ms. Duke also recently resisted White House pressure to write a letter endorsing Ms. Nielsen, one of the people said. Ms. Nielsen worked for Mr. Kelly when he was Mr. Trump's first Homeland Security secretary, and followed him to the White House when he was named chief of staff in July.

The Washington Post first reported that the White House pressured Ms. Duke to end the protected status for tens of thousands of Honduran immigrants living in the United States.

In their discussions on Monday, Ms. Duke, who was Mr. Trump's choice in January to be deputy homeland security secretary, also told Mr. Kelly she would resign from the department once Ms. Nielsen was confirmed, two of the people familiar with the calls said. The Senate Homeland Security committee held a confirmation hearing for Ms. Nielsen on Wednesday but has delayed its vote on her nomination while senators seek more information from her, a Senate aide said.

The immigration program, known as Temporary Protected Status, was enacted by Congress in 1990 to protect foreigners, particularly Central Americans, fleeing war, natural disasters or catastrophes and was extended to Haitians after the 2010 earthquake. About 300,000 people are enrolled.

The Trump administration will have to make similar decisions about Haitian immigrants later this month and El Salvadorans in March. The Nicaraguans who were protected under the program have until January 2019 to leave the United States.

In a news release on Monday night, Ms. Duke said that despite getting information from a number of different sources regarding Honduras, she needed extra time to determine if ground conditions in the country warranted sending people back. She extended the temporary protective status for Hondurans until July 5, 2018.

A memo written by the department's Office of International Affairs division suggested extending the temporary protective status for another 18 months, saying it made no sense to send citizens of Honduras, Nicaragua and El Salvador who were covered back to their countries of origin.

The memo suggested that economies in those countries were still incapable of creating sufficient job opportunities for their young and growing populations and could not handle an influx of thousands of returning people.

"We are still years away from a Central America in which people see their futures at home and not in the United States," the memo read, according to people who saw the document.

Over all, the decision to end the program received pushback from other officials at the department, Homeland Security employees said.

In response to questions about pressure to end the program, they said, White House officials and Mr. Kelly were making the argument to Ms. Duke that conditions had improved enough in Honduras to allow the protected immigrants to return home.

MICHAEL D. SHEAR contributed reporting.

Stoking Fears, Trump Defied Bureaucracy to Advance Immigration Agenda

BY MICHAEL D. SHEAR AND JULIE HIRSCHFELD DAVIS | DEC. 23, 2017

The changes have had far-reaching consequences, both for the immigrants who have sought to make a new home in this country and for America's image in the world.

WASHINGTON — Late to his own meeting and waving a sheet of numbers, President Trump stormed into the Oval Office one day in June, plainly enraged.

Five months before, Mr. Trump had dispatched federal officers to the nation's airports to stop travelers from several Muslim countries from entering the United States in a dramatic demonstration of how he would deliver on his campaign promise to fortify the nation's borders. But so many foreigners had flooded into the country since January, he vented to his national security team, that it was making a mockery of his pledge. Friends were calling to say he looked like a fool, Mr. Trump said.

According to six officials who attended or were briefed about the meeting, Mr. Trump then began reading aloud from the document, which his domestic policy adviser, Stephen Miller, had given him just before the meeting. The document listed how many immigrants had received visas to enter the United States in 2017. More than 2,500 were from Afghanistan, a terrorist haven, the president complained.

Haiti had sent 15,000 people. They "all have AIDS," he grumbled, according to one person who attended the meeting and another person who was briefed about it by a different person who was there. Forty thousand had come from Nigeria, Mr. Trump added. Once they had seen the United States, they would never "go back to their huts" in Africa, recalled the two officials, who asked for anonymity to discuss a sensitive conversation in the Oval Office.

As the meeting continued, John F. Kelly, then the secretary of homeland security, and Rex W. Tillerson, the secretary of state, tried to interject, explaining that many were short-term travelers making one-time visits. But as the president continued, Mr. Kelly and Mr. Miller turned their ire on Mr. Tillerson, blaming him for the influx of foreigners and prompting the secretary of state to throw up his arms in frustration. If he was so bad at his job, maybe he should stop issuing visas altogether, Mr. Tillerson fired back.

Tempers flared and Mr. Kelly asked that the room be cleared of staff members. But even after the door to the Oval Office was closed, aides could still hear the president berating his most senior advisers. Sarah Huckabee Sanders, the White House press secretary, denied on Saturday morning that Mr. Trump had made derogatory statements about immigrants during the meeting.

"General Kelly, General McMaster, Secretary Tillerson, Secretary Nielsen and all other senior staff actually in the meeting deny these outrageous claims," she said, referring to the current White House chief of staff, the national security adviser and the secretaries of state and homeland security. "It's both sad and telling The New York Times would print the lies of their anonymous 'sources' anyway."

While the White House did not deny the overall description of the meeting, officials strenuously insisted that Mr. Trump never used the words "AIDS" or "huts" to describe people from any country. Several participants in the meeting told Times reporters that they did not recall the president using those words and did not think he had, but the two officials who described the comments found them so noteworthy that they related them to others at the time.

The meeting in June reflects Mr. Trump's visceral approach to an issue that defined his campaign and has indelibly shaped the first year of his presidency.

Seizing on immigration as the cause of countless social and economic problems, Mr. Trump entered office with an agenda of symbolic but incompletely thought-out goals, the product not of rigorous policy debate but of emotionally charged personal interactions and an instinct for tapping into the nativist views of white working-class Americans.

Like many of his initiatives, his effort to change American immigration policy has been executed through a disorderly and dysfunctional process that sought from the start to defy the bureaucracy charged with enforcing it, according to interviews with three dozen current and former administration officials, lawmakers and others close to the process, many of whom spoke on the condition of anonymity to detail private interactions.

But while Mr. Trump has been repeatedly frustrated by the limits of his power, his efforts to remake decades of immigration policy have gained increasing momentum as the White House became more disciplined and adept at either ignoring or undercutting the entrenched opposition of many parts of the government. The resulting changes have had far-reaching consequences, not only for the immigrants who have sought to make a new home in this country, but also for the United States' image in the world.

"We have taken a giant steamliner barreling full speed," Mr. Miller said in a recent interview. "Slowed it, stopped it, begun to turn it around and started sailing in the other direction."

It is an assessment shared ruefully by Mr. Trump's harshest critics, who see a darker view of the past year. Frank Sharry, the executive director of America's Voice, a pro-immigration group, argues that the president's immigration agenda is motivated by racism. "He's basically saying, 'You people of color coming to America seeking the American dream are a threat to the white people,' " said Mr. Sharry, an outspoken critic of the president. "He's come into office with an aggressive strategy of trying to reverse the demographic changes underway in America."

A PLEDGE WITH APPEAL

Those who know Mr. Trump say that his attitude toward immigrants long predates his entry into politics. "He's always been fearful where

Mr. Trump's campaign promises included building a wall — and making Mexico pay for it — as well as barring Muslims from entering the country.

other cultures are concerned and always had anxiety about food and safety when he travels," said Michael D'Antonio, who interviewed him for the biography "The Truth About Trump." "His objectification and demonization of people who are different has festered for decades."

Friends say Mr. Trump, a developer turned reality TV star, grew to see immigration as a zero-sum issue: What is good for immigrants is bad for America. In 2014, well before becoming a candidate, he tweeted: "Our government now imports illegal immigrants and deadly diseases. Our leaders are inept." But he remained conflicted, viewing himself as benevolent and wanting to be liked by the many immigrants he employed.

Over time, the anti-immigrant tendencies hardened, and two of his early advisers, Roger J. Stone Jr. and Sam Nunberg, stoked that sentiment. But it was Mr. Trump who added an anti-immigrant screed to his Trump Tower campaign announcement in June 2015 in New York City without telling his aides.

"When do we beat Mexico at the border? They're laughing at us, at our stupidity," Mr. Trump ad-libbed. "They're sending people that have lots of problems, and they're bringing those problems," he continued. "They're bringing drugs; they're bringing crime; they're rapists."

During his campaign, he pushed a false story about Muslims celebrating in Jersey City as they watched the towers fall after the Sept. 11, 2001, attacks in New York. He said illegal immigrants were like "vomit" crossing the border. And he made pledges that he clearly could not fulfill. "We will begin moving them out, Day 1," he said at a rally in August 2016, adding, "My first hour in office, those people are gone."

Democrats and some Republicans recoiled, calling Mr. Trump's messaging damaging and divisive. But for the candidate, the idea of securing the country against outsiders with a wall had intoxicating appeal, though privately, he acknowledged that it was a rhetorical device to whip up crowds when they became listless.

Senator Tom Cotton, Republican of Arkansas, whom Mr. Trump consults regularly on the matter, said it was not a stretch to attribute Mr. Trump's victory to issues where Mr. Trump broke with a Republican establishment orthodoxy that had disappointed anti-immigrant conservatives for decades. "There's no issue on which he was more unorthodox than on immigration," Mr. Cotton said.

BAN RESTARTS ENFORCEMENT

Mr. Trump came into office with a long list of campaign promises that included not only building the wall (and making Mexico pay for it), but creating a "deportation force," barring Muslims from entering the country and immediately deporting millions of immigrants with criminal records.

Mr. Miller and other aides had the task of turning those promises into a policy agenda that would also include an assault against a pro-immigration bureaucracy they viewed with suspicion and disdain.

Working in secret, they drafted a half-dozen executive orders. One would crack down on so-called sanctuary cities. Another proposed changing the definition of a criminal alien so that it included people arrested — not just those convicted.

But mindful of his campaign promise to quickly impose "extreme vetting," Mr. Trump decided his first symbolic action would be an executive order to place a worldwide ban on travel from nations the White House considered compromised by terrorism.

With no policy experts in place, and deeply suspicious of career civil servants they regarded as spies for President Barack Obama, Mr. Miller and a small group of aides started with an Obama-era law that identified seven terror-prone "countries of concern." And then they skipped practically every step in the standard White House playbook for creating and introducing a major policy.

The National Security Council never convened to consider the travel ban proposal. Sean Spicer, the White House press secretary at the time, did not see it ahead of time. Lawyers and policy experts at the White House, the Justice Department and the Homeland Security Department were not asked to weigh in. There were no talking points for friendly surrogates, no detailed briefings for reporters or lawmakers, no answers to frequently asked questions, such as whether green card holders would be affected.

The announcement of the travel ban on a Friday night, seven days after Mr. Trump's inauguration, created chaotic scenes at the nation's largest airports, as hundreds of people were stopped, and set off widespread confusion and loud protests. Lawyers for the government raced to defend the president's actions against court challenges, while aides struggled to explain the policy to perplexed lawmakers the next night at a black-tie dinner. White House aides resorted to Google searches and frenzied scans of the United States Code to figure out which countries were affected.

But for the president, the chaos was the first, sharp evidence that he could exert power over the bureaucracy he criticized on the campaign trail. "It's working out very nicely," Mr. Trump told reporters in the Oval Office the next day.

At a hastily called Saturday night meeting in the Situation Room, Mr. Miller told senior government officials that they should tune out the whining. Sitting at the head of the table, across from Mr. Kelly, Mr. Miller repeated what he told the president: This is what we wanted — to turn immigration enforcement back on. Mr. Kelly, who shared Mr. Trump's views about threats from abroad, was nonetheless livid that his employees at homeland security had been called into action with no guidance or preparation. He told angry lawmakers that responsibility for the rollout was "all on me." Privately, he told the White House, "That's not going to happen again."

FORCED TO BACK DOWN

Amid the turbulent first weeks, Mr. Trump's attempt to bend the government's immigration apparatus to his will began to take shape. The ban's message of "keep out" helped drive down illegal border crossings as much as 70 percent, even without being formally put into effect.

Immigration officers rounded up 41,318 undocumented immigrants during the president's first 100 days, nearly a 40 percent increase. The Justice Department began hiring more immigration judges to speed up deportations. Officials threatened to hold back funds for sanctuary cities. The flow of refugees into the United States slowed.

Mr. Trump "has taken the handcuffs off," said Steven A. Camarota of the Center for Immigration Studies, an advocacy group that favors more limits on immigration. Mr. Obama had been criticized by immigrant rights groups for excessive deportations, especially in his first term. But Mr. Camarota said that Mr. Trump's approach was "a distinct change, to look at what is immigration doing to us, rather than what is the benefit for the immigrant."

The president, however, remained frustrated that the shift was not yielding results. By early March, judges across the country had blocked his travel ban. Immigrant rights activists were crowing that they had thwarted the new president. Even Mr. Trump's own lawyers told him he had to give up on defending the ban.

Attorney General Jeff Sessions and lawyers at the White House and Justice Department had decided that waging an uphill legal battle to defend the directive in the Supreme Court would fail. Instead, they wanted to devise a narrower one that could pass legal muster. The president, though, was furious about what he saw as backing down to politically correct adversaries. He did not want a watered-down version of the travel ban, he yelled at Donald F. McGahn II, the White House counsel, as the issue came to a head on Friday, March 3, in the Oval Office.

It was a familiar moment for Mr. Trump's advisers. The president did not mind being told "no" in private, and would sometimes relent. But he could not abide a public turnabout, a retreat. At those moments, he often exploded at whoever was nearby.

As Marine One waited on the South Lawn for Mr. Trump to begin his weekend trip to Palm Beach, Fla., Mr. McGahn insisted that administration lawyers had already promised the court that Mr. Trump would issue a new order. There was no alternative, he said. "This is bullshit," the president responded.

With nothing resolved, Mr. Trump, furious, left the White House. A senior aide emailed a blunt warning to a colleague waiting aboard Air Force One at Joint Base Andrews in Maryland: "He's coming in hot." Already mad at Mr. Sessions, who the day before had recused himself in the Russia investigation, Mr. Trump refused to take his calls. Aides told Mr. Sessions he would have to fly down to Mar-a-Lago to plead with the president in person to sign the new order.

Over dinner that night with Mr. Sessions and Mr. McGahn, Mr. Trump relented. When he was back in Washington, he signed the new order. It was an indication that he had begun to understand — or at least, begrudgingly accept — the need to follow a process. Still, one senior adviser later recalled never having seen a president so angry signing anything.

As a candidate, Mr. Trump had repeatedly contradicted himself about the deportations he would pursue, and whether he was opposed to any kind of path to citizenship for undocumented immigrants. But he also courted conservative voters by describing an Obama-era policy as an illegal amnesty for the immigrants who had been brought to the United States as children.

During the transition, his aides drafted an executive order to end the program, known as Deferred Action for Childhood Arrivals. But the executive order was held back as the new president struggled with conflicted feelings about the young immigrants, known as Dreamers. "We're going to take care of those kids," Mr. Trump had pledged to Senator Richard J. Durbin during a private exchange at his Inauguration Day luncheon. The comment was a fleeting glimpse of the president's tendency to seek approval from whoever might be sitting across from him, and the power that personal interactions have in shaping his views.

In 2013, Mr. Trump met with a small group of Dreamers at Trump Tower, hoping to improve his standing with the Hispanic community. José Machado told Mr. Trump about waking up at the age of 15 to find his mother had vanished — deported, he later learned, back to Nicaragua. "Honestly," Mr. Machado said of Mr. Trump, "he had no idea."

Mr. Trump appeared to be touched by the personal stories, and insisted that the Dreamers accompany him to his gift shop for watches, books and neckties to take home as souvenirs. In the elevator on the way down, he quietly nodded and said, "You convinced me."

Aware that the president was torn about the Dreamers, Jared Kushner, his son-in-law, quietly reached out in March to Mr. Durbin, who had championed legislation called the Dream Act to legalize the immigrants, to test the waters for a possible deal.

After weeks of private meetings on Capitol Hill and telephone conversations with Mr. Durbin and Senator Lindsey Graham, a South Carolina Republican supportive of legalizing the Dreamers, Mr. Kushner invited them to dinner at the six-bedroom estate he shares with his wife, Ivanka Trump.

But Mr. Durbin's hope of a deal faded when he arrived to the house and saw who one of the guests would be. "Stephen Miller's presence made it a much different experience than I expected," Mr. Durbin said later.

CONFRONTING THE 'DEEP STATE'

Even as the administration was engaged in a court battle over the travel ban, it began to turn its attention to another way of tightening the border — by limiting the number of refugees admitted each year to the United States. And if there was one "deep state" stronghold of Obama holdovers that Mr. Trump and his allies suspected of undermining them on immigration, it was the State Department, which administers the refugee program.

At the department's Bureau of Population, Refugees and Migration, there was a sense of foreboding about a president who had once warned that any refugee might be a "Trojan horse" or part of a "terrorist army."

Mr. Trump had already used the travel ban to cut the number of allowable refugees admitted to the United States in 2017 to 50,000, a fraction of the 110,000 set by Mr. Obama. Now, Mr. Trump would have to decide the level for 2018.

At an April meeting with top officials from the bureau in the West Wing's Roosevelt Room, Mr. Miller cited statistics from the restrictionist Center for Immigration Studies that indicated that resettling refugees in the United States was far costlier than helping them in their own region.

Mr. Miller was visibly displeased, according to people present, when State Department officials pushed back, citing another study that found refugees to be a net benefit to the economy. He called the contention absurd and said it was exactly the wrong kind of thinking.

But the travel ban had been a lesson for Mr. Trump and his aides on the dangers of dictating a major policy change without involving the people who enforce it. This time, instead of shutting out those officials, they worked to tightly control the process.

In previous years, State Department officials had recommended a refugee level to the president. Now, Mr. Miller told officials the number would be determined by the Department of Homeland Security under a new policy that treated the issue as a security matter, not a diplomatic one.

When he got word that the Office of Refugee Resettlement had drafted a 55-page report showing that refugees were a net positive to the economy, Mr. Miller swiftly intervened, requesting a meeting to discuss it. The study never made it to the White House; it was shelved in favor of a three-page list of all the federal assistance programs that refugees used.

At the United Nations General Assembly in September, Mr. Trump cited the Center for Immigration Studies report, arguing that it was more cost-effective to keep refugees out than to bring them into the United States.

"Uncontrolled migration," Mr. Trump declared, "is deeply unfair to both the sending and receiving countries."

MORE DISCIPLINED APPROACH

Cecilia Muñoz, who served as Mr. Obama's chief domestic policy adviser, said she was alarmed by the speed with which Mr. Trump and his team have learned to put their immigration agenda into effect.

"The travel ban was a case of bureaucratic incompetence," she said. "They made rookie mistakes. But they clearly learned from that experience. For the moment, all of the momentum is in the direction of very ugly, very extreme, very harmful policies."

By year's end, the chaos and disorganization that marked Mr. Trump's earliest actions on immigration had given way to a more disciplined approach that yielded concrete results, steered in large part by Mr. Kelly, a retired four-star Marine general. As secretary of homeland security, he had helped unleash immigration officers who felt constrained under Mr. Obama. They arrested 143,000 people in 2017, a sharp uptick, and deported more than 225,000.

Later, as White House chief of staff, Mr. Kelly quietly persuaded the president to drop his talk of Mexico paying for the wall. But he has advocated on behalf of the president's restrictionist vision, defying his reputation as a moderator of Mr. Trump's hard-line instincts.

In September, a third version of the president's travel ban was issued with little fanfare and new legal justifications. Then, Mr. Trump overruled objections from diplomats, capping refugee admissions at 45,000 for 2018, the lowest since 1986. In November, the president ended a humanitarian program that granted residency to 59,000 Haitians since a 2010 earthquake ravaged their country.

As the new year approached, officials began considering a plan to separate parents from their children when families are caught entering the country illegally, a move that immigrant groups called draconian.

At times, though, Mr. Trump has shown an openness to a different approach. In private discussions, he returns periodically to the idea of a "comprehensive immigration" compromise, though aides have warned him against using the phrase because it is seen by his core supporters as code for amnesty. During a fall dinner with Democratic leaders, Mr. Trump explored the possibility of a bargain to legalize Dreamers in exchange for border security.

Mr. Trump even told Republicans recently that he wanted to think bigger, envisioning a deal early next year that would include a wall, protection for Dreamers, work permits for their parents, a shift to merit-based immigration with tougher work site enforcement, and ultimately, legal status for some undocumented immigrants. The idea would prevent Dreamers from sponsoring the parents who brought them illegally for citizenship, limiting what Mr. Trump refers to as "chain migration."

"He wants to make a deal," said Mr. Graham, who spoke with Mr. Trump about the issue last week. "He wants to fix the entire system." Yet publicly, Mr. Trump has only employed the absolutist language that defined his campaign and has dominated his presidency. After an Uzbek immigrant was arrested on suspicion of plowing a truck into a bicycle path in Lower Manhattan in October, killing eight people, the president seized on the episode.

Privately, in the Oval Office, the president expressed disbelief about the visa program that had admitted the suspect, confiding to a group of visiting senators that it was yet another piece of evidence that the United States' immigration policies were "a joke."

Even after a year of progress toward a country sealed off from foreign threats, the president still viewed the immigration system as plagued by complacency. "We're so politically correct," he complained to reporters in the cabinet room, "that we're afraid to do anything."

Trump Sets Up a Grand Bargain on Immigration

OPINION | BY GEORGE J. BORJAS | FEB. 2, 2018

TO END THE POLARIZED and paralyzed debate over immigration policy, President Trump has proposed a deal. The president will grant amnesty to an estimated 1.8 million so-called Dreamers — young people who were brought illegally to the United States as children — in return for (a) $25 billion for a wall on the southern border and other border enforcement measures; (b) elimination of the lottery that distributes 50,000 visas per year, with a reallocation of some of those visas to high-skilled immigrants; and (c) curbing chain migration by "limiting family sponsorship to spouses and minor children only."

Not surprisingly, advocates on both sides have argued that this is a terrible deal: A wall is un-American and won't work anyway; the planned limits on chain migration are racist; and granting amnesty gives the wrong set of incentives to potential immigrants abroad.

Another problem with the proposal, though, may be that it is not bold enough in dealing with the full expanse of our immigration policy.

Those who argue that the wall won't work have something of a point. Although a wall is a mighty symbol, and symbols matter, it's far from clear that a wall would stop illegal immigration. Nearly half of the illegal immigrants are visa overstayers; they might land at Kennedy Airport or Los Angeles International Airport with, say, a tourist visa, then overstay the visa and quickly disappear in this big country.

The only way to truly curtail illegal immigration may require that all employers use an electronic system like E-Verify to certify the legal status of newly hired workers, accompanied by sizable penalties for employers who break the law.

Those who argue that getting rid of chain migration is racist are just throwing scare words into the fire to choke debate. Our current system lets a new immigrant eventually sponsor the entry of her

Demonstrators gathered at the Capitol in January in support of so-called Dreamers.

brother, who can then sponsor the entry of his wife, who can sponsor her father, who can sponsor his sister, and so on. Does it really make sense for one entry today to eventually lead to a visa for the immigrant's sister-in-law's aunt?

Finally, President Trump's proposal attempts to bring some economic sense into immigration policy. It would get rid of the lottery and reallocate some of those visas to high-skilled workers. This is a step in the right direction, as long as we care about the economic benefits from immigration. But the reallocation of fewer than 50,000 visas would barely make a dent.

Perhaps a bigger objection is the three big issues it leaves off the table, and perhaps bringing those issues back into the realm of the possible would allow for a better deal.

The debate over illegal immigration will not end if Congress enacts the president's proposal. If the government grants amnesty to nearly two million Dreamers, there will still be at least nine million illegal immigrants left behind "in the shadows." Would anyone be surprised if there were then continuing discussions about how to package the plight of those nine million illegal immigrants in a way that highlighted their suffering and that forced politicians to pay immediate attention to their situation?

Those who have a gut reaction against regularizing the status of nine million illegal immigrants may need to bite the bullet. Their reluctance is understandable — our last attempt at an amnesty, in 1986, failed, and did not solve the problem. But there is little appetite, and rightly so, for deporting nine million people. Most of those immigrants have been our neighbors for many years, have stayed out of legal trouble and have deep roots in our communities. Perhaps bringing them into the debate today would let us reach a better solution to the festering immigration problem.

The second issue not on the table is the realignment of policy for legal immigration on an economically rational basis. Last summer, two Republican senators, Tom Cotton of Arkansas and David Perdue of Georgia, proposed a point system in which potential immigrants would be "graded" on the basis of their education, age and English-language skills, and those who passed the test would be granted admission. This type of point system is precisely what other immigrant-receiving countries like Canada and Australia do.

And, finally, there is the numbers issue. Exactly how many immigrants should be let in? We now admit about one million legal immigrants a year. The limits on chain migration might cut the numbers by about 400,000 and would closely align with the recommendation of the 1997 immigration commission led by the legendary Barbara Jordan, which suggested a flow of 550,000 legal immigrants a year.

The widespread dissatisfaction with immigration, and the political and economic consequences that reverberate throughout our country, suggest that the current numbers are not sustainable. The open borders crowd may also have to bite the bullet. Most Americans have no appetite for even the current levels of immigration.

So let's put everything on the table, including the legal status of the millions of illegal immigrants who entered the country as adults and changing immigration policy in a way that is more economically beneficial. But let's also be realistic and acknowledge up front that the road to a deal is going to be very bumpy.

The number of illegal immigrants who would eventually qualify for an amnesty, whether they are Dreamers or not, will probably be much larger than current estimates suggest. Back in 1986, one provision of the Immigration Reform and Control Act was expected to grant amnesty to 400,000 farm workers. In fact, 1.1 million applied. When California granted illegal immigrants the opportunity to get a driver's license in 2013, Department of Motor Vehicles offices were swamped, with illegal immigrants coming in at twice the expected rate.

Any attempt at limiting chain migration creates a new problem. There is a waiting list of about 3.9 million chain-migration applicants, and many have waited years for the golden ticket. Amazingly enough, some potential immigrants from the Philippines have been waiting since Oct. 1, 1994. Many people will think that we need to grandfather in those applicants. But that would require temporary rules that might allow, say, 400,000 immigrants per year until the queue was cleared out.

We should also be skeptical of claims that an amnesty to millions of illegal immigrants, many of whom have little schooling, or even just to the Dreamers, who typically have a high school diploma, will be an economic boon. The amnesty is going to be expensive. The Congressional Budget Office estimates that the net cost of granting amnesty to the Dreamers (the additional expenses minus the taxes they pay) would run to $25 billion over the next 10 years. An amnesty will be far costlier if it is extended to the entire illegal population, which is less skilled on average.

So the first step in any deal will be — must be — securing the border. A deal where enforcement is the first priority ensures that illegal immigration will be greatly curtailed, and this provision alone may well be worth its weight in gold. Past administrations, both Democratic and Republican, looked the other way as illegal immigration graduated from a relatively minor problem (the 1986 immigration act granted amnesty to fewer than three million illegal immigrants) into a major distortion of the immigration system.

A sensible immigration policy that generates economic benefits for Americans and for immigrants already here ensures that we can better adapt to the economic shocks that will visit us in the next few decades. And the best way to maximize those benefits is to filter the pool of persons who want to migrate.

Before jumping in to claim that such "filtering" is un-American, it's worth remembering that anything short of open borders inevitably involves filtering. Between the 1920s and 1965, the filtering was done through national origin, giving preference to immigrants born in Western European countries. Since 1965, we have preferred immigrants who have relatives already living here. Filtering on the basis of economic potential ensures that immigration generates the largest possible economic gain for our country.

There is some concern that whatever deal the Trump administration reaches will be easily undone by the next administration. I'm not so sure this is a valid point. History teaches us that it is extremely difficult to change immigration policy. The stars aligned only twice in the past century: once in the 1920s and then again in the 1960s.

Given the nature of the policy shifts that some politicians tried to ram through under the label "comprehensive immigration reform," it is not surprising that the label became loaded and maligned. Nevertheless, President Trump's proposal opens the door for a truly comprehensive attempt at simultaneously tackling all the big issues that confront us.

Let's build on what the president has proposed and address the lingering problems in a way where the benefits and the costs are shared by all those who have a stake in the system, immigrant and native-born alike.

GEORGE BORJAS is a professor of economics and social policy at the Harvard Kennedy School and the author of, most recently, "We Wanted Workers: Unraveling the Immigration Narrative."

Is America a 'Nation of Immigrants'? Immigration Agency Says No

BY MIRIAM JORDAN | FEB. 22, 2018

LOS ANGELES — The federal agency that issues green cards and grants citizenship to people from foreign countries has stopped characterizing the United States as "a nation of immigrants."

The director of United States Citizenship and Immigration Services informed employees in a letter on Thursday that its mission statement had been revised to "guide us in the years ahead." Gone was the phrase that described the agency as securing "America's promise as a nation of immigrants."

The original mission statement, created in 2005, said,: "U.S.C.I.S. secures America's promise as a nation of immigrants by providing accurate and useful information to our customers, granting immigration and citizenship benefits, promoting an awareness and understanding of citizenship, and ensuring the integrity of our immigration system."

The new version says: "U.S. Citizenship and Immigration Services administers the nation's lawful immigration system, safeguarding its integrity and promise by efficiently and fairly adjudicating requests for immigration benefits while protecting Americans, securing the homeland and honoring our values."

The agency director, L. Francis Cissna, who was appointed by the Trump administration, described the revision as a "simple, straightforward statement" that "clearly defines the agency's role in our country's lawful immigration system and the commitment we have to the American people."

Mr. Cissna did not mention in his letter that he had removed the phrase "nation of immigrants," which was popularized by a book by President John F. Kennedy and is frequently used to convey America's multiculturalism.

However, Mr. Cissna did note that he had eliminated the word "customers" in describing the foreign nationals whom the agency serves, "a reminder that we are always working for the American people."

León Rodríguez, director of the agency from 2014 to 2017, said the revision of the mission statement marked "a particularly sad turn of history." "We should not forget that under the discarded mission statement, the integrity and national security functions of U.S.C.I.S. grew — dramatically so — showing that we could be both a welcoming nation and a safe one," Mr. Rodríguez said. "We should stop to reflect about the many opportunities that America will lose because of the attitudes reflected in this statement, and ask ourselves whether this is really the country we want to be."

Ira Mehlman, a spokesman for the Federation for American Immigration Reform, which favors restricting immigration, applauded the change. "A nation of immigrants isn't a mission statement," he said, "it's a slogan." "The biggest problem with our immigration system is that it lacks a clear national interest objective," he added.

As director of U.S.C.I.S., Mr. Cissna has promoted an agenda that reflects the Trump administration's skeptical and often hard-line stance on immigration. The agency has increased scrutiny of visa applications for foreign workers whom American companies seek to hire; it has changed the asylum application process to discourage people from seeking safe haven in the United States; and it has added steps to the process for foreigners already in the country to obtain legal permanent residency, or a green card.

U.S.C.I.S., a unit of the Department of Homeland Security, reviews petitions of foreign nationals who seek to visit, work, reside and find refuge in the United States. It also processes citizenship applications, which have surged since President Trump won the election in 2016.

In his letter to his staff, Mr. Cissna wrote, "We are also responsible for ensuring that those who naturalize are dedicated to this country, share our values, assimilate into our communities, and understand their responsibility to help preserve our freedom and liberty."

Published posthumously, Kennedy's "A Nation of Immigrants" highlighted the contribution of immigrants when the country was engulfed in a debate over the direction of its immigration policy. The phrase appears at least as far back as 1874, in an editorial published in The Daily State Journal of Alexandria, which praised a bill passed by the Virginia Senate appropriating $15,000 to encourage European immigration. "We are a nation of immigrants and immigrants' children," it said.

Immigrant advocates today invoke the phrase to remind the country that most Americans have an ancestor who was once a newcomer to the United States.

A Twitter Rant That Rails and Misleads on Immigration Policy

BY LINDA QIU | APRIL 3, 2018

IN A DOZEN Twitter missives over the past three days, President Trump has accused Democrats of failing to protect young undocumented immigrants, criticized Mexico for its role in illegal immigration to the United States and warned of "caravans" of people headed toward the southern border.

At least half of his statements were inaccurate. Here's a fact-check.

Mr. Trump warned that new immigrants would take advantage of DACA, and said that Democrats were responsible for the program's demise.

This is not possible in the first case and false in the second.

These big flows of people are all trying to take advantage of
DACA. They want in on the act!

— Donald J. Trump (@realDonaldTrump) Apr. 1, 2018

In several tweets, Mr. Trump referred to "caravans" of immigrants headed toward the United States' southern border. Buzzfeed has reported that hundreds of Central Americans are walking en masse through Mexico, staying together for protection from cartels and immigration authorities. Organizers estimated that up to 10 to 15 percent of the migrants would seek asylum at the United States border.

But to qualify for DACA, or Deferred Action for Childhood Arrivals, the immigrants would have had to have been living in the United States since 2007. Furthermore, in September Mr. Trump rescinded the program, which shielded immigrants who arrived in the United States illegally as children from deportation.

Though the program's fate is tied up in court, American immigration officials are not accepting new applications. A White House official said Mr. Trump was referring to a bipartisan Senate bill that would have extended applicants' eligibility to 2012 from 2007. It also directed the Department of Homeland Security to prioritize deporting criminals.

The bill failed in the Republican-controlled Senate. But even if it had become law, immigrants entering the United States today would still not qualify.

DACA is dead because the Democrats didn't care or act, and now everyone wants to get onto the DACA bandwagon... No longer works. Must build Wall and secure our borders with proper Border legislation. Democrats want No Borders, hence drugs and crime!

— Donald J. Trump (@realDonaldTrump) Apr. 2, 2018

Several states won injunctions in January and February requiring the federal government to accept applications from current DACA recipients to renew their resident status. On Tuesday, citing data from United States Citizenship and Immigration Services, Attorney General Xavier Becerra of California estimated that at least 30,000 of the so-called Dreamers have been able to renew their DACA status since January.

It's also misleading to claim that the Democrats did not act to renew DACA, as The New York Times reported last month:

Democratic leaders have rejected Mr. Trump's demand to pair the program with funding for a border wall, but that is not nearly the same as not wanting a legislative solution at all.

Democrats met with Mr. Trump and Republican lawmakers in January to discuss a deal, during which Senator Dianne Feinstein, Democrat of California, suggested a "clean DACA bill." At the meeting, Mr. Trump agreed.

But hours later, the White House said Mr. Trump's concept of a "clean DACA bill" included border security. Negotiations stalled, and weeks later, Democrats briefly shut down the government over the issue.

In February, Representative Nancy Pelosi of California, the House Democratic leader, delivered an eight-hour speech about the plight of the young undocumented immigrants known as Dreamers. The Congressional

Hispanic Caucus, in a letter dated Feb. 28, said Mr. Trump had "thwarted every bipartisan, narrow agreement that seeks to provide relief for Dreamers" and listed a few examples.

And this week, several Democratic lawmakers who voted no on the spending bill said they did so because it did not contain protections for Dreamers.

He accused Mexico of doing nothing to address illegal immigration but said the country had "strong border laws."

These tweets contradict each other and require context.

Mexico is doing very little, if not NOTHING, at stopping people from flowing into Mexico through their Southern Border, and then into the U.S. They laugh at our dumb immigration laws. They must stop the big drug and people flows, or I will stop their cash cow, NAFTA. NEED WALL!

— Donald J. Trump (@realDonaldTrump) Apr. 1, 2018

Mexico is making a fortune on NAFTA...They have very strong border laws - ours are pathetic. With all of the money they make from the U.S., hopefully they will stop people from coming through their country and into ours, at least until Congress changes our immigration laws!

— Donald J. Trump (@realDonaldTrump) Apr. 2, 2018

Mr. Trump first chastised Mexico for not preventing Central American migrants from reaching the United States. But a day later, he praised Mexico for its "strong border laws."

Though some advocacy groups and researchers have found that Mexico's approach to curbing illegal immigration is ineffective, the country is not doing "nothing."

The Mexican government adopted its Programa Frontera Sur, or southern border program, in 2014 to protect migrants and the country's ports of entry. Assessments from Rice University and the Washington Office on Latin America found that Mexico has had success detaining and deporting migrants, but failed to protect migrant rights or adopt a comprehensive strategy for long-term solutions.

He repeatedly referred to Nafta as a "cash cow" for Mexico.

This is exaggerated.

The big Caravan of People from Honduras, now coming across Mexico and heading to our "Weak Laws" Border, had better be stopped before it gets there. Cash cow NAFTA is in play, as is foreign aid to Honduras and the countries that allow this to happen. Congress MUST ACT NOW!

— Donald J. Trump (@realDonaldTrump) Apr. 3, 2018

A White House official said Mr. Trump was referring to Mexican exports that enter the United States tax-free because of the North American Free Trade Agreement.

But most United States exports to Mexico are also exempted from tariffs and other trade barriers.

More broadly, Mr. Trump's characterization of Nafta as a "cash cow" for Mexico is wrong. Most research has found that Nafta has had a positive, but modest, net impact on Mexico's economy.

It is true that the pact helped increase Mexico's trade globally. Since Nafta went into effect in 1994, Mexico's foreign direct investment has drastically increased, its manufacturing sector has become more productive, and it has generally widened trade with the rest of the world.

But economists also say Nafta hasn't produced the robust growth that was expected. The Mexican economy has grown at slower average rates than elsewhere Latin America. Poverty and unemployment are stagnant. The Mexican wage gap with the United States has grown instead of shrunk. And critics argue that Nafta has hurt the Mexican agricultural sector, leading to farming job losses.

The president excoriated the so-called catch-and-release immigration enforcement policy as an example of "ridiculous liberal (Democrat) laws."

This is false.

Border Patrol Agents are not allowed to properly do their job at the Border because of ridiculous liberal (Democrat) laws like Catch & Release. Getting more dangerous. "Caravans" coming. Republicans must go to Nuclear Option to pass tough laws NOW. NO MORE DACA DEAL!

— Donald J. Trump (@realDonaldTrump) Apr. 1, 2018

"Catch and release" refers to the practice of paroling detained immigrants as they wait for courts to determine whether they should be deported. The Supreme Court has ruled that unauthorized immigrants who have been ordered to be deported generally cannot be detained for more than six months. Women and children who are held together must be released within 21 days under a separate 2016 federal court ruling that minors cannot be held for extended periods.

There is also not enough detention space to house captured immigrants. In the 2017 fiscal year, for example, Immigration and Customs Enforcement detained a daily average of about 38,000 people, but had only 34,000 beds available for the majority of the year. (Congress funded 5,300 additional beds in May, with four months left in the 2017 fiscal year.)

In October, Attorney General Jeff Sessions said a backlog of cases was contributing to the release of immigrants. "There is so many people claiming and being entitled to hearings that we don't have the ability to provide those hearings, and they're being released into the community and they're not coming back for their hearings," he said.

Additionally, the government already turns away far more people who are stopped at or near the border — and are not subjected to lengthy court proceedings — than unauthorized immigrants who are caught within the United States.

Asked to explain Mr. Trump's tweet, the White House provided a February fact sheet from the Department of Homeland Security that focused mostly on unaccompanied immigrant children. It concluded that only 3.5 percent of the unaccompanied minors were eventually deported, and blamed a 1997 court settlement and a 2008 law for creating "legal loopholes" permitting their release from detention.

The 1997 case dates to the Reagan administration. It was settled under the Clinton administration to ensure humane treatment and care of unaccompanied minors when their cases are processed by the federal government. Laws passed in 2002 and 2008, under President George W. Bush, then divided the responsibilities for apprehension and care of unaccompanied children among federal agencies.

CHAPTER 2

Who Should Go?

When it comes to immigrants, both illegal and legal, the
threat of deportation is constant. The legal system and
the Immigration and Customs Enforcement agency (known
as ICE) decide whether immigrants should be deported,
regardless of whether they came to the United States
to seek asylum from human rights violations or escape
natural disasters. Who should be allowed to stay, even if
they entered illegally, and who should be forced to leave?
Law enforcement officials face this question every day.

New Trump Deportation Rules Allow Far More Expulsions

BY MICHAEL D. SHEAR AND RON NIXON | FEB. 21, 2017

WASHINGTON — President Trump has directed his administration to
enforce the nation's immigration laws more aggressively, unleashing
the full force of the federal government to find, arrest and deport those
in the country illegally, regardless of whether they have committed
serious crimes.

Documents released on Tuesday by the Department of Homeland
Security revealed the broad scope of the president's ambitions: to pub-
licize crimes by undocumented immigrants; strip such immigrants of
privacy protections; enlist local police officers as enforcers; erect new
detention facilities; discourage asylum seekers; and, ultimately, speed
up deportations.

The new enforcement policies put into practice language that Mr.
Trump used on the campaign trail, vastly expanding the definition of

"criminal aliens" and warning that such unauthorized immigrants "routinely victimize Americans," disregard the "rule of law and pose a threat" to people in communities across the United States.

Despite those assertions in the new documents, research shows lower levels of crime among immigrants than among native-born Americans.

The president's new immigration policies are likely to be welcomed by some law enforcement officials around the country, who have called for a tougher crackdown on unauthorized immigrants, and by some Republicans in Congress who have argued that lax enforcement encourages a never-ending flow of unauthorized immigrants.

But taken together, the new policies are a rejection of the sometimes more restrained efforts by former Presidents Barack Obama and George W. Bush and their predecessors, who sought to balance protecting the nation's borders with fiscal, logistical and humanitarian limits on the exercise of laws passed by Congress.

"The faithful execution of our immigration laws is best achieved by using all these statutory authorities to the greatest extent practicable," John F. Kelly, the secretary of homeland security, wrote in one of two memorandums released on Tuesday. "Accordingly, department personnel shall make full use of these authorities."

The immediate impact of that shift is not yet fully known. Advocates for immigrants warned on Tuesday that the new border control and enforcement directives would create an atmosphere of fear that was likely to drive those in the country illegally deeper into the shadows.

Administration officials said some of the new policies — like one seeking to send unauthorized border crossers from Central America to Mexico while they await deportation hearings — could take months to put in effect and might be limited in scope.

For now, so-called Dreamers, who were brought to the United States as young children, will not be targeted unless they commit crimes, officials said on Tuesday.

Mr. Trump has not yet said where he will get the billions of dollars needed to pay for thousands of new border control agents, a network of detention facilities to detain unauthorized immigrants and a wall along the entire southern border with Mexico.

But politically, Mr. Kelly's actions on Tuesday serve to reinforce the president's standing among a core constituency — those who blame unauthorized immigrants for taking jobs away from citizens, committing heinous crimes and being a financial burden on federal, state and local governments.

And because of the changes, millions of immigrants in the country illegally now face a far greater likelihood of being discovered, arrested and eventually deported.

"The message is: The immigration law is back in business," said Mark Krikorian, the executive director of the Center for Immigration Studies, which supports restricted immigration. "That violating immigration law is no longer a secondary offense."

Lawyers and advocates for immigrants said the new policies could still be challenged in court. Maricopa County in Arizona spent years defending its sheriff at the time, Joseph Arpaio, in federal court, where he was found to have discriminated against Latinos.

And courts in Illinois, Oregon, Pennsylvania and several other states have rejected the power given to local and state law enforcement officers to hold immigrants for up to 48 hours beyond their scheduled release from detention at the request of federal authorities under a program known as Secure Communities, which Mr. Trump is reviving.

"When you tell state and local police that their job is to do immigration enforcement," said Omar Jadwat, director of the American Civil Liberties Union's Immigrants' Rights Project, "it translates into the unwarranted and illegal targeting of people because of their race, because of their language, because of the color of their skin."

Sean Spicer, the White House press secretary, said on Tuesday that the president wanted to "take the shackles off" of the nation's immigration enforcers. He insisted that the new policies made it clear that "the No. 1 priority is that people who pose a threat to our country are immediately dealt with."

In fact, that was already the policy under the Obama administration, which instructed agents that undocumented immigrants convicted of serious crimes were the priority for deportation. Now, enforcement officials have been directed to seek the deportation of anyone in the country illegally.

"Under this executive order, ICE will not exempt classes or categories of removal aliens from potential enforcement," a fact sheet released by the Department of Homeland Security said, using the acronym for Immigration and Customs Enforcement. "All of those present in violation of the immigration laws may be subject to immigration arrest, detention, and, if found removable by final order, removal from the United States."

That includes people convicted of fraud in any official matter before a governmental agency and people who "have abused any program related to receipt of public benefits."

The policy also expands a program that lets officials bypass due process protections such as court hearings in some deportation cases.

Under the Obama administration, the program, known as "expedited removal," was used only when an immigrant was arrested within 100 miles of the border and had been in the country no more than 14 days. Now it will include all those who have been in the country for up to two years, no matter where they are caught.

"The administration seems to be putting its foot down as far as the gas pedal will go," said Heidi Altman, policy director for the National Immigrant Justice Center, a Chicago-based group that offers legal services to immigrants.

In the documents released on Tuesday, the Department of Homeland Security is directed to begin the process of hiring 10,000 immigration and customs agents, expanding the number of detention facilities and creating an office within Immigration and Customs Enforcement to help families of those killed by undocumented immigrants.

The directives would also revive a program that recruits local police officers and sheriff's deputies to help with deportation, effectively making them de facto immigration agents. The effort, called the 287(g) program, was scaled back during the Obama administration.

The program faces resistance from many states and dozens of so-called sanctuary cities, which have refused to allow their law enforcement workers to help round up undocumented individuals. In New York, Mayor Bill de Blasio in a statement on Tuesday pledged the city's cooperation in cases involving "proven public safety threats," but vowed that "what we will not do is turn our N.Y.P.D. officers into immigration agents."

Under the new directives, the agency would no longer provide privacy protections to people who are not American citizens or green card holders. A policy established in the last days of the Bush administration in January 2009 provided some legal protection for information collected by the Department of Homeland Security on nonresidents.

The new policies also target unauthorized immigrants who smuggle their children into the country, as happened with Central American children seeking to reunite with parents living in the United States. Under the new directives, such parents could face deportation or prosecution for smuggling or human trafficking.

Officials said that returning Central American refugees to Mexico to await hearings would be done only in a limited fashion, and only after discussions with the government of Mexico.

Mexican officials said on Tuesday that such a move could violate Mexican law and international accords governing repatriation, and immigrants' advocates questioned Mexico's ability to absorb thousands of Central Americans in detention centers and shelters.

Reporting was contributed by **LIZ ROBBINS**, **VIVIAN YEE** and **CAITLIN DICKERSON** from New York; **KIRK SEMPLE** from Mexico City; **FERNANDA SANTOS** from Phoenix; and **LINDA QIU** from Washington.

Only Mass Deportation Can Save America

OPINION | BY BRET STEPHENS | JUNE 16, 2017

IN THE MATTER of immigration, mark this conservative columnist down as strongly pro-deportation. The United States has too many people who don't work hard, don't believe in God, don't contribute much to society and don't appreciate the greatness of the American system.

They need to return whence they came.

I speak of Americans whose families have been in this country for a few generations. Complacent, entitled and often shockingly ignorant on basic points of American law and history, they are the stagnant pool in which our national prospects risk drowning.

On point after point, America's nonimmigrants are failing our country. Crime? A study by the Cato Institute notes that nonimmigrants are incarcerated at nearly twice the rate of illegal immigrants, and at more than three times the rate of legal ones. Educational achievement? Just 17 percent of the finalists in the 2016 Intel Science Talent Search — often called the "Junior Nobel Prize" — were the children of United States-born parents. At the Rochester Institute of Technology, just 9.5 percent of graduate students in electrical engineering were nonimmigrants.

Religious piety — especially of the Christian variety? More illegal immigrants identify as Christian (83 percent) than do Americans (70.6 percent), a fact right-wing immigration restrictionists might ponder as they bemoan declines in church attendance.

Business creation? Nonimmigrants start businesses at half the rate of immigrants, and accounted for fewer than half the companies started in Silicon Valley between 1995 and 2005. Overall, the share of nonimmigrant entrepreneurs fell by more than 10 percentage points between 1995 and 2008, according to a Harvard Business Review study.

Nor does the case against nonimmigrants end there. The rate of out-of-wedlock births for United States-born mothers exceeds the rate for foreign-born moms, 42 percent to 33 percent. The rate of delinquency and criminality among nonimmigrant teens considerably exceeds that of their immigrant peers. A recent report by the Sentencing Project also finds evidence that the fewer immigrants there are in a neighborhood, the likelier it is to be unsafe.

And then there's the all-important issue of demographics. The race for the future is ultimately a race for people — healthy, working-age, fertile people — and our nonimmigrants fail us here, too. "The increase in the overall number of U.S. births, from 3.74 million in 1970 to 4.0 million in 2014, is due entirely to births to foreign-born mothers," reports the Pew Research Center. Without these immigrant moms, the United States would be faced with the same demographic death spiral that now confronts Japan.

Bottom line: So-called real Americans are screwing up America. Maybe they should leave, so that we can replace them with new and better ones: newcomers who are more appreciative of what the United States has to offer, more ambitious for themselves and their children, and more willing to sacrifice for the future. In other words, just the kind of people we used to be — when "we" had just come off the boat.

O.K., so I'm jesting about deporting "real Americans" en masse. (Who would take them in, anyway?) But then the threat of mass deportations has been no joke with this administration. On Thursday, the Department of Homeland Security seemed prepared to extend an Obama administration program known as Deferred Action for Childhood Arrivals, or DACA, which allows the children of illegal immigrants — some 800,000 people in all — to continue to study and work in the United States. The decision would have reversed one of Donald Trump's ugly campaign threats to deport these kids, whose only crime was to have been brought to the United States by their parents.

Yet the administration is still committed to deporting their parents, and on Friday the D.H.S. announced that even DACA remains under review — another cruel twist for young immigrants wondering if they'll be sent back to "home" countries they hardly ever knew, and whose language they might barely even speak.

Beyond the inhumanity of toying with people's lives this way, there's also the shortsightedness of it. We do not usually find happiness by driving away those who would love us. Businesses do not often prosper by firing their better employees and discouraging job applications. So how does America become great again by berating and evicting its most energetic, enterprising, law-abiding, job-creating, idea-generating, self-multiplying and God-fearing people?

Because I'm the child of immigrants and grew up abroad, I have always thought of the United States as a country that belongs first to its newcomers — the people who strain hardest to become a part of it because they realize that it's precious; and who do the most to remake it so that our ideas, and our appeal, may stay fresh.

That used to be a cliché, but in the Age of Trump it needs to be explained all over again. We're a country of immigrants — by and for them, too. Americans who don't get it should get out.

Prosecutors' Dilemma: Will Conviction Lead to 'Life Sentence of Deportation'?

BY VIVIAN YEE | JULY 31, 2017

THE DRUNKEN-DRIVING case seemed straightforward, the kind that prosecutors in Seattle convert into a quick guilty plea hundreds of times a year: a swerving car, a blood-alcohol level more than twice the legal limit, a first-time offense that caused no injuries.

The only complication was the driver. A 23-year-old undocumented immigrant studying at the University of Washington, she had gained some assurance against deportation through a federal program for people who had entered the country illegally as children. If she pleaded guilty to driving under the influence, the punishment any Washington resident might face could be compounded by a more permanent penalty. She could lose her protected status; she could be deported. Which, for the prosecutor, presented a difficulty: Was this what justice should look like?

Now that President Trump's hard line has made deportation a keener threat, a growing number of district attorneys are coming to the same reckoning, concluding that prosecutors should consider potential repercussions for immigrants before closing a plea deal. At the same time, cities and states are reshaping how the criminal justice system treats immigrants, hoping to hopscotch around any unintended immigration pitfalls.

These shifts may inaugurate yet another local-versus-federal conflict with the Trump administration, which is already tussling with many liberal cities over other protections for immigrants.

For prosecutors, such policies are also stretching, if not bursting, the bounds of the profession. Justice is supposed to be blind to the identity of a defendant. But, the argument goes, the stakes might warrant a peek. "There's certainly a line of argument that says, 'Nope, we're not going to consider all your individual circumstances, we want to treat everybody the same,' " said Dan Satterberg, the prosecuting attorney for Seattle and a longtime Republican, who instituted an immigration-consequences policy last year and strengthened it after the presidential election. "But more and more, my eyes are open that treating people the same means that there isn't a life sentence of deportation that might accompany that conviction."

With that in mind, his office allowed the student to plead guilty to reckless driving instead of driving under the influence. The deal, which included three days of community service and two years of probation — milder than the standard driving-under-the-influence penalty of 24 hours in jail, a few days' community service and five years' probation — did not jeopardize her protected status.

But many prosecutors remain wary, hesitant to meddle in what they regard as the federal government's business and even more reluctant to depart from what they say is a bedrock principle of the system.

"There's probably hundreds if not thousands of issues that I suppose we could take into consideration," said Brian McIntyre, the county attorney in Cochise County, Ariz., "and when we do that, we necessarily wind up not being as fair to someone else."

Cochise prosecutors are not supposed to consider the collateral effects of a conviction, whether it be to a child custody case or a military career. If he made accommodations for an immigrant, Mr. McIntyre said, he felt that he would also owe a citizen in similar circumstances the same option, "because is he not being, essentially, negatively impacted by his U.S. citizenry?"

A criminal record often has different stakes for an immigrant than it does for a citizen. It can mean losing a green card or being barred from citizenship. Those who lack legal status can lose any chance to gain it. Those with legal status, as well as those without, can face automatic deportation.

In many cases, the city-and-state-level changes dovetail with broader criminal justice reforms that were already underway before Mr. Trump took office. But to the administration, policies that help noncitizens duck immigration penalties are tantamount to an assault on the rule of law. "It troubles me that we've seen district attorneys openly brag about not charging cases appropriately under the laws of our country," Attorney General Jeff Sessions said in April.

The local efforts to help immigrants may not always work. The Trump administration has made clear that anyone without legal status may be deported, regardless of whether they have been convicted of a crime. But reducing criminal penalties can help immigrants by keeping them out of jail, which can make it more difficult for Immigration and Customs Enforcement to find them, or by preserving their options in immigration court.

In May, Denver stopped imposing a maximum jail sentence of 365 days for some lower-level crimes, like shoplifting. A conviction with a potential sentence of a year or longer — even if the actual sentence is far shorter — can disqualify noncitizens from most forms of legal status or render them deportable. "Whether you committed a physical assault on someone or were caught urinating in the park, you were subject to the same maximum penalties, which doesn't make sense," the mayor, Michael B. Hancock, said in an interview.

The Denver shift builds on state laws in California and Washington State that cap misdemeanor penalties at 364 days. That ceiling applies retroactively in California, a major benefit for people detained by the immigration authorities over old convictions. Immigration lawyers say they frequently see immigrants stripped of green cards or visas over convictions for lower-level crimes, exposing them to deportation.

"Not only do you do your time and pay your fine under criminal court," said Jeannette Zanipatin, a lawyer at the Mexican American Legal Defense and Educational Fund, "but you're literally banished from your family and everyone you know."

In some states, interventions have come from as high up as the governor's mansion. In recent months, Democratic governors in Colorado, Virginia and New York have tried to help immigrants facing deportation by pardoning their old crimes, though the results have been mixed. One was released after a pardon, but another has been deported and a third remains detained.

Prosecutors who take immigration status into account say this consideration will not be extended to serious or violent crimes. They argue that showing flexibility in nonviolent, minor cases will help build trust with immigrants in their communities, making them more likely to report crimes and serve as witnesses.

The acting Brooklyn district attorney, Eric Gonzalez, went further than most in April, when he announced that his prosecutors would begin notifying defense lawyers about the potential immigration fallout of their clients' cases and that he would hire two in-house immigration lawyers to consult on prosecutions.

Days later, the state's attorney for Baltimore, Marilyn J. Mosby, said she had told her staff members to use their discretion when it came to cases with an immigration factor, considering defendants' prior records and community ties. "There's no set standard," she said. "You have to base it on everything that's in front of you."

It is not yet clear what that will look like in Baltimore or Brooklyn. But in Santa Clara County, Calif., whose district attorney was among the first to outline an official policy, prosecutors often allow a noncitizen to plead guilty to a lesser charge in exchange for more jail time or probation. "If we're giving something, we're going to get something," said the district attorney, Jeff Rosen.

California law now requires immigration consequences to be factored into criminal cases. The state has also passed a law allowing people to erase or revise old convictions if they successfully argue that they were not advised at the time that a guilty or no-contest plea would endanger their immigration status.

Occasionally, cases involving noncitizens have boomeranged on local officials. In April, Mr. Rosen's office was plunged into a controversy surrounding a domestic-violence case in which a green-card holder from India was charged with felony domestic violence against his wife, a citizen, but ultimately pleaded guilty to lesser charges. The woman has criticized the plea deal as too lenient. Although prosecutors considered the potential loss of the man's green card in negotiations, Mr. Rosen said, they felt there was not enough evidence to prove the initial charges in court.

In Boston, a suspect in the double murder of two physicians in May, a legal resident from Guinea-Bissau, had been able to keep his green card despite robbing two banks in recent years after his lawyer negotiated a plea deal that allowed him to plead to larceny instead of unarmed bank robbery. The sentence he received from a judge was also one day short of the 365-day threshold that could have led to his deportation.

But backlash has been infrequent, and prosecutors have continued to take immigrants' status into account. Luke Larson, the deputy prosecutor on the case of the Washington State student charged with drunken driving, said several factors favored a milder charge, including her strong academic record and lack of a criminal history. Most unsettling, for him, was that she had not been back to her home country since she was a toddler. She got the deal.

"It's easier to say, 'I don't want to know about the potential immigration consequences, and I don't care,' " said his boss, Mr. Satterberg. "It's harder when you want to know. Then it does require you to know more and to be more creative and to take more of a risk with the case."

A Game of Cat and Mouse
With High Stakes: Deportation

BY LIZ ROBBINS | AUG. 3, 2017

THERE'S A NEW GAME afoot. The federal government's current emphasis on deporting undocumented immigrants — even those facing low-level charges — has, in effect, turned courthouses in New York State into arenas where practitioners of criminal law face off against enforcers of immigration law.

In New York City, judges, defense lawyers and clients have been on high alert for months, watching to see if immigration enforcement officers, many in plainclothes, are in a courthouse. If a pair of people look suspicious, lawyers from the Bronx Defenders, Brooklyn Defender Services and the Legal Aid Society send an internal email alert. Defendants duck into bathrooms or race to another floor.

When officers for United States Immigration and Customs Enforcement, known as ICE, are thought to be in a courthouse, a sympathetic judge might reschedule a defendant's appearance, or, in a seemingly perverse move, set bail that could send a defendant to Rikers Island — keeping the person out of ICE's hands because the jail complex does not turn over undocumented immigrants to the agency.

"I don't want to be playing the cat and mouse game with federal authorities," Eric Gonzalez, the acting Brooklyn district attorney, said in an interview.

State policy prohibits ICE officers from making arrests inside courtrooms. They must do their work in a hallway or outside a building. But on Thursday, Mr. Gonzalez and Eric T. Schneiderman, the state attorney general, held a news conference to say that even that was too much and that ICE should treat courthouses as sensitive locations — like hospitals, houses of worship and schools — where it does not make arrests. They said immigration authorities were interfering with the criminal justice system, making witness and defendants afraid to appear in court.

SAM HODGSON FOR THE NEW YORK TIMES

Eric Gonzalez, the acting Brooklyn district attorney, left, and Eric T. Schneiderman, New York's attorney, at a news conference where they discussed immigration officials picking up defendants at courthouses.

"I am asking ICE to reconsider their policy and treat the courthouse with respect," Mr. Gonzalez said in the interview.

ICE has said that it goes to courthouses because it is safer than trying to detain someone at home or on the street. Sarah Rodriguez, the agency's spokeswoman, said that despite the demand by the New York officials, "ICE plans to continue arresting individuals in courthouse environments as necessary, based on operational circumstances."

Ms. Rodriguez said that those picked up by ICE "often have significant criminal histories." ICE officers have made 53 arrests in or around courts in New York State since January, compared to 11 arrests in 2016 and 14 in 2015, according to the Immigrant Defense Project, an advocacy group. Thirty-five of the arrests were made in or around city courthouses, including one on Thursday in Brooklyn.

The state Office of Court Administration said there were 52 instances of ICE officials identifying themselves to court officers; they made 30 arrests, 25 of which occurred in the city. The office did not keep statistics in previous years.

The number of ICE arrests in the five boroughs is higher than other areas in the state because jails in most counties are allowed to hand over prisoners to ICE. While there are no numbers that suggest either defendants or witnesses are staying away from court, and thus impeding trials, Mr. Gonzalez said his office's ability to prosecute cases was nonetheless affected: "Witnesses are not willing to come forward and cooperate."

Mr. Gonzalez added that ICE's arrests had undermined the trust people have in the justice system. The Immigrant Defense Project said that, based on reports from lawyers, some of those recently arrested were charged with offenses like driving without a license or disorderly conduct and that one young man facing "minor charges" in juvenile court in Suffolk County had been seized.

Under the Obama administration, undocumented immigrants with those types of arrests or convictions were not a priority for deportation, but President Trump has made clear that all people in the country illegally are targets.

Jessica M. Vaughan, director of policy studies for the Center for Immigration Studies, which favors more controls on immigration, said in an email that the issue was not that ICE is interfering with the criminal justice system, but that New York's so-called sanctuary policies "are interfering with ICE's ability to carry out its legitimate and important mission. They are the ones forcing ICE to resort to courtroom arrests."

The clash over authority was evident recently at the Queens Human Trafficking Intervention Court, where women charged with prostitution are supposed to face restorative, not punitive, justice. Those arrested can take part in counseling sessions in exchange for dismissal of their charges and the sealing of the records. Undocumented immigrants may be eligible for visas as victims.

On June 16, ICE officers went to the court looking for several individuals, including a 29-year-old woman from China who had been

Judge Toko Serita, shown in 2014, recently set bail for a woman accused of prostitution; the woman was then able to speak to her lawyer without being arrested by ICE.

charged with unlicensed practice of massage and prostitution; she had overstayed her tourist visa.

Court officers, as per union policy, told Judge Toko Serita that ICE officers were in the hallway near the courtroom. She told the defense counsel and the assistant district attorney. Judge Serita set bail at $500 and the woman was held in the jail behind the courtroom — with Rikers Island her ultimate destination — where she met with her lawyer. Later that afternoon, Judge Serita released the defendant on her own recognizance. The ICE agents had left, apparently in search of another target.

Judge Serita said she had not set bail for the purpose of evading the law. "It's to give the individual an opportunity to discuss the matter with his or her lawyer," she said. As it happened, ICE officers arrested another woman as she left the court and was walking toward the subway, her lawyer, Sheldon Glass, said. Rachael Yong

Yow, a spokeswoman for the New York ICE field office, confirmed the arrest.

Following that action, Chief Judge Janet DiFiore met with federal immigration authorities and asked ICE to consider the trafficking court as a sensitive location. The policy remains.

Not all judges are sympathetic. Tiffany Gordon, a Legal Aid lawyer in the Bronx, said that a case involving one of her clients had gone before four judges, and there had been different reactions to the suggestion that federal agents might be in the courthouse.

The man, a 38-year-old undocumented immigrant from Ecuador, was charged with driving while impaired and was afraid to show up to his first appearance because he thought ICE would be at the courthouse. Agents were, indeed, there.

Ms. Gordon said that the judge that day, Bahaati Pitt, asked for a reason to reschedule; Ms. Gordon offered that she was busy with other cases. The judge accepted that answer. The next appearance, however, was before Judge Beth Beller. Again, ICE agents were in the courthouse to arrest the man, but he was waiting them out at a nearby McDonald's. Judge Beller issued a bench warrant, compelling him to appear, which he did not do that day.

"She wasn't going to assist us in navigating around it," Ms. Gordon said. She got her client excused from his next two court dates, with two other judges. Judge Beller declined to comment because the case is still active.

Lawyers cannot tell their clients not to show up. "We cannot ethically advise them not to go to court," Lee Wang, a lawyer with the Immigrant Defense Project, said. Instead, she added, lawyers look to be creative.

Asking a judge to set bail for a client to go to Rikers is an extreme measure, but according to Ms. Wang it happened six times since January when ICE was present. Two of those times, the judges refused.

"What does it mean that they will be safer in Rikers than being released?" Ms. Wang asked. "I think it means we're in an ugly place."

About 2,500 Nicaraguans to Lose Special Permission to Live in U.S.

BY RON NIXON | NOV. 6, 2017

WASHINGTON — Thousands of immigrants from Nicaragua who came to the United States illegally, many of them decades ago, will lose special permission allowing them to stay in the country, the Trump administration said on Monday.

However, officials from the Department of Homeland Security said the effective date of termination would be delayed one year, until Jan. 5, 2019, to give about 2,500 individuals time to leave the country or adjust their immigration status.

The program allowing them to stay, Temporary Protected Status, was enacted by Congress in 1990 to protect foreigners, particularly Central Americans, fleeing war, natural disasters or catastrophes and was extended to Haitians after the 2010 earthquake.

Officials said that Elaine Duke, the acting secretary of homeland security, had not made a decision on hundreds of thousands of immigrants from Haiti, El Salvador and Honduras who are also covered under the program. The department had until Monday to extend or terminate the program for Nicaragua and Honduras. Ms. Duke, saying she did not have enough information, said she would continue to review protections for Hondurans. The temporary protective status covering immigrants from Honduras will be extended for at least six months, through July 5.

The Trump administration said that in some cases, the protection for foreigners has stretched into decades, and the Departments of State and Homeland Security decided that the living conditions in their home countries had improved enough for them to return. The administration and some allied lawmakers, including Senator Charles E. Grassley, Republican of Iowa, said the immigrants received public benefits and took jobs that might otherwise be filled by unemployed American citizens.

Many of the more than 300,000 people shielded from deportation under the program have lived in the United States for years and bought homes, embarked on careers and given birth to children who are American citizens.

Now they face an uncertain future.

People protected under the program will be given six months to leave after their current permissions expire. The temporary status for the 86,000 Hondurans and 5,000 Nicaraguans in the program expires in early January, and Monday was the deadline for the Department of Homeland Security to decide whether to renew that status. It has until Thanksgiving to decide whether to extend the protection for thousands of Haitians. The program covers 10 countries: El Salvador, Haiti, Honduras, Nepal, Nicaragua, Somalia, Sudan, South Sudan, Syria and Yemen.

The Trump administration's decisions to rescind the temporary protection status for Nicaraguans is part of its effort to reduce both legal and illegal immigration to the United States. The administration has moved aggressively to enforce the nation's immigration laws, arresting and deporting those in the country illegally, regardless of whether they have committed serious crimes and reducing the number of refugees.

Democratic members of Congress and advocates called the move inhumane. Senator Benjamin L. Cardin, Democrat of Maryland, said that sending tens of thousands of people back to Central American nations still recovering from natural disasters or internal strife could destabilize those countries. In a statement, Mr. Cardin said the effort was part of the "White House's radical anti-immigration agenda," which ignored an honest assessment of conditions in each of the countries.

A coalition of immigration groups also criticized the Trump administration for ending the protection. "The Trump administration's recommendation to terminate temporary protected status for hundreds of thousands of people from all over the globe living in the United States is cruel and shameful," Steven Choi, the executive director for the New

York Immigration Coalition, said at a news conference on Monday in New York. "America will not be greater or safer by sending back people who've made their lives here."

Belinda Osorio, 48, who arrived in 1991 in the United States from Honduras seeking work, said she was relieved the news had not been as bad as she had feared. She had read and heard that her temporary protected status would be cut off immediately.

Still, it was only a postponement of the panic that was to come.

"I don't think six months is going to fix anything because what are we going to do after six months?" said Ms. Osorio, a housekeeper at one of the Disney World resort hotels in Orlando, Fla. "We're not going to leave. I'm not going to leave my country. I'm not going to take my kids to a dangerous country."

She said that she was afraid that if they were forced to return to Honduras, her 14-year-old son would be forced to join a violent gang. Her 72-year-old mother has been threatened by gang members who have demanded money from her, and Ms. Osorio said she feared she and her children, as returnees from the United States, would have it even worse.

Like many other recipients of temporary protected status, Ms. Osorio built a life here expecting that she would not be forced to return anytime soon. She had married an American citizen, another hotel employee, with whom she had two children; it was through her job that her family had medical insurance. For years, she said, she had been trying to apply for a green card based on her marriage, and she hoped she would succeed before the temporary program expired.

"At least I have hope with my husband, but there's a lot of people, they don't have nothing. Their only hope is T.P.S.," she said. "It's not fair after so many years working so hard in this country, and they just want to get rid of us just like that."

John F. Kelly, the former secretary of homeland security and now the White House chief of staff, had extended temporary protected status for Haitians in May, giving them an additional six months to stay in the country.

Salvadorans, who make up about 60 percent of those in the Temporary Protected Status program, were first granted protection in March 2001 after a series of earthquakes in the country. Their protective status will expire next year, on March 9. The status is renewed periodically, and recipients have to keep their permits updated to avoid deportation, paying $495 each time. The Obama administration typically granted 18-month waivers.

Last week, a bipartisan group of lawmakers led by Representatives Carlos Curbelo and Ileana Ros-Lehtinen, Republicans of Florida, and Representatives Frederica S. Wilson and Alcee L. Hastings, Democrats of Florida, introduced a bill that would try to provide permanent legal status for some Haitians, Nicaraguans, Salvadorans and Hondurans.

Being Deported From Home for the Holidays

BY DAVID GONZALEZ | NOV. 26, 2017

LIANY AND MARIA VILLACIS grew up in a family that did everything together. Each summer, even when money was tight, their parents made sure to take a week's vacation, no matter how modest. Last summer, when Liany, 22, was in a finance training program in Chicago, her parents and twin sister took their family vacation in the Windy City.

Their closeness was a result of circumstance as much as blood: The twins were born in Pasto, Colombia, where their mother, Liany Guerrero, hailed from a politically active family. But when they started receiving death threats from rebel groups — along with unsettling snapshots of the girls at play — they sought political asylum in 2001 in New York with their father, Juan Villacis, whose mother lived in the Woodhaven section of Queens.

They paid their taxes and stayed out of trouble. The twins prospered and did well in school and college. And every year, when the parents went to see the authorities at Immigration and Customs Enforcement to renew their stay of removal, they went as a family.

After this year's meeting, they came home one short.

On Nov. 15, Juan was detained and sent to the Bergen County Jail in New Jersey to await deportation to his native Ecuador in the coming weeks. His wife was allowed to go home, but under supervision and with orders to return this week to prove she has purchased a one-way ticket back to Colombia for mid-January. Their lawyer, Jillian Hopman, was stunned by what she saw as a heartless bureaucracy going after low-hanging fruit rather than the "bad hombres" of legend.

"For a family that does everything together, this is heartbreaking," Ms. Hopman said. "Juan's mother's health has seriously deteriorated, and he is the one who cares for her. His wife has all kinds of medical problems, including complex cysts in her breasts. ICE did not care

Liany Guerrero, center, with her twin daughters, Liany Villacis, left, and Maria Villacis, right, on the porch of their home in Queens.

about any of this. Juan could have won the Nobel Prize and taken a bullet for Mike Pence. All he has become is a statistic."

Adding to the sting, immigration officers refused to let the twins or his wife give him a final hug goodbye, Ms. Hopman said. "They told us they no longer provide that courtesy," she said, "because they don't like emotional scenes." Rachael Yong Yow, a spokeswoman for the immigration agency, did not respond to questions submitted last week by email.

Liany Guerrero and Juan Villacis met in Quito, Ecuador, Juan's hometown, where both were studying physical therapy. They have been married 29 years. In Pasto, Liany had served as a first lady of sorts when her older brother was mayor. The family had been politically active and had been targets of rebel groups. One relative had been kidnapped. It was an obvious — if difficult — decision to seek asylum in New York when the threats against the family stepped up in the late 1990s.

Maria said her family arrived with valid visas in 2001 and immediately sought political asylum. However, she said, their lawyer at the time stressed the family's social class — rather than political affiliation — as the reason they were targeted by rebels. Although their application was denied, they obtained stays of removal every year. Ms. Hopman took their case in 2010.

The twins did not expect things to go awry this year: Their father's mother, a United States citizen who is confined to bed and in poor health, has applied for him to become a legal resident, but there is nearly a five-year backlog of cases. Their mother's health makes the situation critical, too, they thought.

Instead, their lawyer emerged with bad news. "My mom went completely pale and held onto her knees," said Liany, who with her sister has protection for now under DACA, the Deferred Action for Childhood Arrivals program. "She was just staring at the floor, saying there had to be a mistake."

Friends of the family agree. Alberto Roig, a retired Manhattan prosecutor who also was assistant counsel to former Commissioner Raymond W. Kelly of the New York Police Department, was dumbstruck by the prospect that the family he has known for years would be broken up.

"They're not some schmoes," he said. "The girls are incredible because the parents are incredible. They are contributing to our society. They follow the law. They're legit. And what do we do, kick them out and slam the door? This is a tremendous injustice."

Now is the time of year when Juan would have hauled out the Christmas decorations and strung up the lights around the porch of the family's Dutch Colonial-style home just off the elevated train on Jamaica Avenue in Queens. Instead, it is dark. Inside, his electric drum kit and saxophone rest against a wall, silent. Just the sight of them moved his wife to tears the day she returned home without him.

"Our family life was broken abruptly," she said. "It's like half of my heart was cut out. We always made the effort to keep our family united. We did everything to educate our daughters. Juan is his mother's only hope. We worked hard and paid taxes. What did we do wrong to deserve this?"

She has prided herself on never missing appointments and doing whatever the authorities asked. One request she has yet to fulfill is buying her ticket to Colombia. "I know I have to get it," she said. "But I have the hope that someone will notice our case and say no, this can't happen. Hope is the last thing you lose."

Immigration Agents Target 7-Eleven Stores in Push to Punish Employers

BY PATRICIA MAZZEI | JAN. 10, 2018

FEDERAL IMMIGRATION AGENTS descended on dozens of 7-Eleven convenience stores across the country before daybreak on Wednesday, arresting undocumented workers and demanding paperwork from managers, in what the Trump administration described as its largest enforcement operation against employers so far.

The sweeps of 98 stores in 17 states, from California to Florida, resulted in 21 arrests, according to United States Immigration and Customs Enforcement, which signaled intensified efforts against businesses that hire unauthorized workers.

"Today's actions send a strong message to U.S. businesses that hire and employ an illegal work force: ICE will enforce the law, and if you are found to be breaking the law, you will be held accountable," Thomas D. Homan, the acting director of the agency, said in a statement.

Mr. Homan, the nation's top immigration-enforcement official, has promised more scrutiny of businesses that knowingly violate federal laws requiring employers to verify the identity and employment eligibility of their workers.

Under President Trump, ICE has significantly expanded immigration enforcement, arresting undocumented immigrants in their homes or when they check in with federal agents as part of immigration court cases.

In a statement, 7-Eleven Inc., based in Irving, Tex., distanced itself from the situation, saying that the individual stores are franchises that belong to independent business owners, who "are solely responsible for their employees, including deciding who to hire and verifying their eligibility to work in the United States."

"7-Eleven takes compliance with immigration laws seriously and has terminated the franchise agreements of franchisees convicted of violating these laws," the company said.

If ICE hoped to make a bold statement, it could hardly pick a more iconic target than 7-Eleven, a chain known for ubiquitous stores that are open all the time and sell the much-loved Slurpees and Big Gulps. Many a 7-Eleven franchise has been a steppingstone for new legal immigrants who want to own and run their own small businesses.

Not all franchisees have been scrupulous about whom they hire. ICE called its Wednesday sweep a "follow-up" of a 2013 investigation that resulted in the arrests of nine 7-Eleven franchise owners and managers on Long Island and in Virginia on charges of employing undocumented workers. Several have pleaded guilty and forfeited their franchises, and have been ordered to pay millions of dollars in back wages owed to the workers.

"This definitely sends a message to employers," said Ira Mehlman, the spokesman for the Federation for American Immigration Reform, which favors more limits on immigration and stricter enforcement.

According to ICE, federal agents served inspection notices to 7-Eleven franchises in California, Colorado, Delaware, Florida, Illinois, Indiana, Maryland, Michigan, Missouri, Nevada, New Jersey, New York, North Carolina, Oregon, Pennsylvania, Texas, Washington State and Washington, D.C.

Employees at two 7-Eleven stores on Staten Island said that immigration agents visited the stores on Wednesday. But the agents were shown valid employment records with Social Security numbers, two workers at each of the stores said, and no one was arrested. In all, 16 of the 98 stores visited on Wednesday were in the New York City area, according to an ICE spokeswoman, Rachael Yong Yow, who would not specify their locations.

In Miami Beach, an employee at one 7-Eleven said that while no agents showed up at her store, her boss asked workers to make sure their employment records were up to date, in case ICE continued its visits. Agents dropped in on 7-Eleven stores in seven cities in southeast Florida, including Miami Beach, according to Nestor Yglesias, an ICE spokesman; he, too, declined to identify specific stores.

Under President George W. Bush, ICE grabbed headlines by rounding up unauthorized workers at meatpacking plants, fruit suppliers, carwashes and residences. In a shift, the agency under President Barack Obama focused on catching border crossers, deporting convicted criminals and pursuing employers on paper, by inspecting the I-9 forms that employers are required to fill out and keep to verify their workers' eligibility.

By targeting 7-Eleven franchisees and their workers on Wednesday, ICE under Mr. Trump appeared to be melding the approaches of his two predecessors: Go after employers while also detaining employees whom agents encountered without work authorization.

One of the biggest workplace immigration raids, in May 2008, resulted in the detention of nearly 400 undocumented immigrants, including several children, at an Iowa meatpacking plant. Sholom Rubashkin, the chief executive of the Agriprocessors plant, which was then the largest kosher meatpacking operation in the country, was eventually convicted of bank fraud in federal court.

President Trump commuted Mr. Rubashkin's 27-year prison sentence last month, after years of lobbying by a number of prominent lawyers and politicians who considered his term unduly harsh, and perhaps even anti-Semitic.

ICE Deportation Cases: Your Questions Answered

BY NIRAJ CHO AND VIVIAN YEE | FEB. 13, 2018

THE DETAILS of their immigration cases in widely shared news stories have elicited public sympathy — a 10-year-old stopped on her way to surgery; another hiding in a church — but they also raise questions about how the nation's complicated immigration policies are enforced.

Take the cases of Syed Ahmed Jamal and Jesus Berrones, which have received a great deal of national attention in recent weeks. Both men have sympathetic stories, faced deportation and received temporary reprieves.

The treatment of people often seems arbitrary and inconsistent. Mr. Jamal, who was detained and separated from his wife and three children in Kansas, received temporary relief despite the efforts of federal authorities to deport him (which continue), while Mr. Berrones, whose 5-year-old son has cancer, was allowed a temporary reprieve on Monday.

The contrast underscores the discretion given to Immigration and Customs Enforcement officials. It also raises questions about the extent of their powers and the rights of detainees. Here are answers to some of those questions.

ARE DEPORTATION ARRESTS MORE COMMON THAN BEFORE?

So far, yes, they are. Between the start of the Trump administration and the end of the 2017 fiscal year, the agency arrested 110,568 people, a 42 percent increase over the same period the year before, according to an ICE report.

WHAT HAPPENS AFTER SOMEONE IS ARRESTED?

It depends. If someone in custody already faces an order of deportation, the options may be limited.

Mr. Jamal and nearly one million others fall into this category. In Mr. Jamal's case, an immigration judge gave him until Oct. 26, 2011, to leave the country voluntarily, according to ICE. When he failed to do so, his departure order became a deportation order.

A lawyer may be able to argue, as Mr. Jamal's successfully did, that the judge should temporarily stay the removal. A lawyer may also be able to persuade a judge to reopen a case if a person's circumstances have changed. But without such a stay, ICE can conclude that the legal process is over and begin deportation as soon as possible, depending on the logistics of sending the individuals to their native country.

That happened to Mr. Jamal on Monday. When his first stay was dissolved, he was placed on a flight. His lawyers said they were able to secure a second stay, however, while his plane was on its way to Hawaii where it would refuel. An individual in custody without such an order of deportation may have more options — and time.

The detainee can apply for asylum or other such programs. Even if that relief isn't available, immigration courts are often backlogged and arrestees have several rounds of appeals to exhaust, a process that can take some time. That said, they may have to spend some or all of that time in detention, where many who lack legal representation simply agree to be deported anyway.

CAN ICE MAKE ARRESTS ANYWHERE?

No. There are two kinds of restrictions on the places where immigration officers can make an arrest: legal and self-imposed. Like other law enforcement agencies, ICE must respect constitutional protections, meaning its officers can't enter a private residence without consent or a warrant, according to Grisel Ruiz, a staff lawyer with the Immigrant Legal Resource Center.

The agency has also vowed on its own to avoid making arrests at "sensitive locations," a policy intended to build trust and allow individuals to engage in some activities "without fear or hesitation." Those include schools, places of worship, hospitals and public demonstrations.

Immigration and Customs Enforcement officers pulling a man over during a traffic stop near his Riverside, Calif., house last summer.

(In response to criticism, ICE recently said it would also put more limits on when it will make arrests in courthouses.)

But that voluntary policy is just that: "It's not binding, it's not law," Ms. Ruiz said. And she and other immigrant advocates say that while the agency may avoid making arrests at those sensitive locations, it continues to arrest people near them.

DOES ICE HAVE TO LET DEPORTEES GET THEIR AFFAIRS IN ORDER?

While they sometimes do, immigration officers are not required to give arrestees the chance to gather their belongings or even say farewell to their loved ones. Mr. Jamal's family said that the officers who arrested him, for example, denied them the right to hug him goodbye. And, often, those being arrested may be far from home and family.

Depending on the stage of the deportation process and criminal history, some individuals are allowed to go free on the condition that they commit to voluntarily leave the country within a specified period.

DO CONTRIBUTIONS TO SOCIETY MAKE ANY DIFFERENCE?

ICE agents are given discretion to decide whether someone should be deported. The agency may let someone stay, under supervision, in extenuating circumstances — if the person is receiving medical treatment or caring for an elderly parent, for example. That appears to have been the case for Mr. Berrones, who reportedly received a one-year stay on his removal that will allow him to continue caring for his ill son. Community pressure, and media attention, has swayed the agency in the past, too.

But, under President Trump, ICE is using that discretion in favor of detainees less often. The administration's position is that anyone who is in the United States illegally is a target for deportation. In the last few years of the Obama administration, on the other hand, agents were told to prioritize some groups, like serious criminals and recent arrivals. So while family, personal circumstances or contributions to society may be considered, they are less likely to help an individual's cause now than they once were.

WHAT ROLE DOES A CRIMINAL RECORD, OR THE LACK OF ONE, PLAY?

The Trump administration considers being in the United States without proper documentation to be a crime, a stricter approach than in the past, when immigration offenses were often thought of more like civil infractions. That means that the agency takes seriously cases in which the only significant mark on someone's record is a failure to comply with a deportation order, as it says was true of Mr. Jamal.

But a lack of a criminal record, apart from immigration offenses, can help to persuade the government to let individuals remain free while they await an administrative decision about their status.

DO YOU GET POINTS FOR TRYING TO ACHIEVE LEGAL STATUS?

While some immigrants, like asylum seekers, are protected from deportation as they await a decision on their status, merely applying does not provide protection. Without a court order or a government commitment to pause deportation, the only thing that matters is a person's current legal status.

But attempts to achieve legal status can help to persuade a judge that an individual need not be detained, says Jesse Lloyd, an Oakland immigration lawyer who is the vice chairman of the American Immigration Lawyers Association's ICE committee. "A history of otherwise complying with immigration authorities is at least a good indication that someone's not a flight risk," he said.

Justice Dept. Restricts a Common Tactic of Immigration Judges

BY KATIE BENNER | MAY 17, 2018

ATTORNEY GENERAL Jeff Sessions issued a directive on Thursday that places limits on a tool commonly used by immigration judges and could put hundreds of thousands of deportation cases that are essentially closed back on federal court dockets.

The move, issued in an interim decision, is unlikely to reopen all the cases. But Mr. Sessions said that immigration courts could not put such cases on indefinite hold by using a practice known as administrative closure, which temporarily removes a case from a judge's calendar and delays a proceeding that could remove an immigrant from the country.

DOUG MILLS/THE NEW YORK TIMES

Attorney General Jeff Sessions with President Trump and Vice President Mike Pence at the National Peace Officers' Memorial Service in May 2018.

Immigration judges "do not have the general authority to suspend indefinitely immigration proceedings by administrative closure," he wrote in the decision, and the practice "effectively resulted in illegal aliens remaining indefinitely in the United States without any formal legal status."

The move injects fresh uncertainty into the lives of undocumented immigrants living in the United States, and some critics say the decision could lead to their deportation before they could gain legal status.

"Sessions is using his authority as attorney general to turn the immigration courts into a deportation assembly line, with ICE officers waiting at the exits with open handcuffs in hand," said David W. Leopold, who oversees the immigration law group at Ulmer & Berne, referring to United States Immigration and Customs Enforcement.

Mr. Sessions, an immigration hard-liner, said that the directive paved the way for such court cases that had been "put 'out of sight, out of mind' " to return to dockets in courts across the country. From October 2011 to last September, 215,285 cases were administratively closed.

But doing so could inundate the court system. "Requiring recalendaring of all of these cases immediately, however, would likely overwhelm the immigration courts and undercut the efficient administration of immigration law," Mr. Sessions wrote.

Given the logistical problems that could follow, the cases could remain closed "unless D.H.S. or the respondent requests recalendaring," he said, referring to the Department of Homeland Security. Critics also expressed concern over the number of cases that could be reopened, saying that the decision eliminated a critical tool that helped ensure the court system would not be bogged down with a huge backlog of cases.

Mr. Sessions dismissed the inherent authority of judges to manage immigration court proceedings "with the stroke of a pen," said Annaluisa Padilla, the president of the American Immigration Lawyers Association.

To address such a backlog, the Justice Department has enacted a plan that includes streamlining its hiring process for judges, increasingly using video teleconferencing to let judges adjudicate cases from around the country and a new electronic filing system.

The Justice Department said Mr. Sessions's opinion eliminated the "unfettered use" of administrative closures and better aligned the immigration system with the rule of law. But Benjamin Johnson, the executive director of the immigration lawyers association, said the directive chipped away at due process. "Due process demands that we maintain an immigration court system with independent judges who have the authority and flexibility to make decisions," Mr. Johnson said.

Immigration advocates also said the practice of administrative closure often offered flexibility. The process is frequently used when an immigrant facing deportation could obtain legal status through another agency, including, for example, whether a person could become eligible for a green card by marrying a United States citizen. The judge may use administrative closure to shelve the case while the Citizenship and Immigration Services evaluates whether the marriage is legitimate. "Administrative closure gives immigration judges critical flexibility and discretion to make fair, due process-based decisions in deportation cases," said Mr. Leopold.

Mr. Sessions has described the country's current immigration policies as a "lawless disgrace."

In March, the Justice Department sued California; Gov. Jerry Brown; and the state's attorney general, Xavier Becerra, over so-called sanctuary laws in the state that the department said were unconstitutional and made it impossible for federal immigration officials to deport criminals who were born outside the United States.

The suit, which asked that the laws be blocked, served as a warning to officials nationwide who have enacted sanctuary policies that offer protections for undocumented immigrants.

What to Expect as the House Heads Toward an Immigration Showdown

BY THOMAS KAPLAN | JUNE 6, 2018

WASHINGTON — Republican lawmakers in the House are hurtling toward a collision over immigration, raising the prospect of a divisive and uncomfortably public intraparty fight just five months before November's midterm elections. And party leaders are running out of time to stop it.

In the face of a rebellion from moderate members, who are on the brink of forcing a series of immigration votes over the objections of Speaker Paul D. Ryan, Republicans will meet privately on Thursday morning to discuss the issue.

"Our members are earnest and sincere in trying to understand each other's perspectives," Mr. Ryan told reporters on Wednesday, adding, "I really do believe that there is a sweet spot here."

At the center of their discussions is the fate of hundreds of thousands of young immigrants brought to the country illegally as children — known as Dreamers. Here's a guide to the impending showdown.

THE FUTURE OF DACA HAS LOOMED FOR MONTHS.

The approaching collision among Republicans has been long in the making. In September, President Trump moved to rescind an Obama-era program that shielded young undocumented immigrants from deportation, known as Deferred Action for Childhood Arrivals, or DACA. He gave Congress six months to take action on the matter.

The Senate tried but came up empty, as three different immigration plans failed in the chamber in February. And because the courts have kept DACA alive for now, lawmakers — who thrive on hard deadlines — have felt less urgency to deal with the issue.

REPUBLICANS ARE DEEPLY DIVIDED.

For months, there have been clear divisions among House Republicans

Representative Kevin McCarthy, the majority leader, and Speaker Paul D. Ryan on their way to a weekly news conference on Capitol Hill in June 2018.

over how to address DACA. Some members have lined up behind a bill sponsored by Representative Robert W. Goodlatte of Virginia, the chairman of the Judiciary Committee, that is intended to appeal to conservatives and sharply reduces legal immigration as well. Others have championed a bill from Representatives Will Hurd, Republican of Texas, and Pete Aguilar, Democrat of California, that has bipartisan support and would provide a path to citizenship for the young undocumented immigrants.

With their members split, House Republican leaders have followed a well-worn path in Congress — they have punted on the issue.

REBELLIOUS MEMBERS EMBRACE A PARLIAMENTARY TACTIC.

Moderate Republicans are tired of waiting. And they are now on the cusp of getting their way.

Republican lawmakers are using what is known as a discharge

petition, which can force floor action over the wishes of House leaders. For the discharge petition to succeed, it needs the signatures of 218 members. By Wednesday, it had 215. Twenty-three Republicans have signed the petition, including members from districts with large Hispanic populations and others who face tough re-election races.

Every Democrat has signed except for Representative Henry Cuellar of Texas, who said he wants a commitment from his party's leadership "saying that they will not support a border wall in exchange for Dreamers."

WHAT COMES NEXT IS HARD TO PREDICT.

Mr. Ryan is no fan of the discharge petition, and he is trying to work with Republican lawmakers on an immigration compromise that could make it unnecessary. Whether moderates and conservatives can find common ground on such a politically challenging issue is unknown. One flash point is the matter of providing young undocumented immigrants with a path to citizenship — and the specifics of what that path would entail.

"We're closer to the magic number to force the issue," said Representative Mario Diaz-Balart of Florida, one of the Republicans who has signed the petition. "But the ideal thing would be if we can have a negotiation that leads to a bill that can pass."

If discussions about an immigration deal fizzle and the discharge petition reaches 218 signatures, it would set up votes this month on four separate immigration plans:

• A proposal put forth by Mr. Goodlatte, presumably a version of his bill.

• A proposal from Representative Lucille Roybal-Allard, Democrat of California. She plans to put forth the Dream Act, a bill that includes a path to citizenship for Dreamers and has widespread support among House Democrats.

- A yet-to-be-revealed proposal put forth by Mr. Ryan.

- A proposal put forth by Representative Jeff Denham, Republican of California, which is expected to be a version of the Hurd-Aguilar bill.

If multiple proposals receive a majority in the House, the one with the greatest number of votes will pass.

A major question mark is how Mr. Trump will respond to any action by the House on immigration. Mr. Trump has called DACA recipients "incredible kids" but has also made steep demands for what must be included in an immigration bill, including wall funding and other hard-line immigration policy changes.

Mr. Trump's reaction is critical. In an interview last month, Senator Mitch McConnell of Kentucky, the majority leader, said he would only return his chamber to the subject of immigration if the House passed a bill that Mr. Trump would sign.

FOR REPUBLICAN LAWMAKERS, RISKS ABOUND.

Immigration is a perilous subject for Republicans, and there is a clear danger for both moderates and conservatives in the days to come.

Moderate lawmakers have shown surprising backbone, but they are a long way from winning the enactment of a law protecting the young undocumented immigrants. If they come up short, those lawmakers could say they tried, but their opponents could point out the bottom line: The fate of DACA recipients is still up in the air.

For conservatives, the thought of a Republican-controlled House passing a bill that they deride as "amnesty" is frightening and could depress Republican turnout in November. "When you mention the A-word," said Representative Mark Meadows, Republican of North Carolina and the chairman of the conservative House Freedom Caucus, "it sends shivers up every conservative's spine."

CHAPTER 3

Debating Who Should Stay and the Dreamers

Deportation affects not only the individuals who are expelled from the United States, but also the loved ones who are left behind on American soil. Immigrants who remain in the United States contend with fear and uncertainty, as well as face challenges in arenas such as immigration courts and sanctuary cities. Dreamers, or undocumented immigrants brought to the United States as minors, face the threat of deportation as the Obama-era Dream Act and DACA are scrutinized under the Trump administration.

The Road, or Flight, From Detention to Deportation

BY FERNANDA SANTOS | FEB. 20, 2017

DURING HIS FRENETIC first week in office, President Trump made good on a core campaign pledge to overhaul the nation's immigration enforcement. With the stroke of a pen, he redefined the meaning of "criminal alien" by vastly expanding the criteria used to decide who is a priority for deportation.

It is not just the "bad hombres" that he talked about on the campaign trail. Any undocumented immigrant convicted of a crime or believed to have committed "acts that constitute a chargeable criminal offense" — essentially, anyone who is suspected of a crime, but has not yet been charged — is now at the top of the list.

For undocumented immigrants, the path between detention and deportation is sometimes long and usually twisted. An immigration judge's deportation order can be appealed — to the Board of Immigration Appeals and, in a very small number of cases, all the way to the Supreme Court.

Field office directors for Immigration and Customs Enforcement, or ICE, can, at their discretion, grant a stay of removal, which is another way of postponing a repatriation. As a federal immigration official put it, "We can put someone in removal proceeding tomorrow and it can take months or years until they reach the finish line."

But what happens once they reach the finish line?

A WILLING DESTINATION

The first step is making sure that the country to which undocumented immigrants are being deported will take them back. Immigration officials must secure a travel document from such a country — essentially a guarantee that it will accept its citizen once that person has been removed from the United States. In most cases, that is not a problem.

Consular officials from Mexico, where a majority of deportees come from, are quick to respond, immigration officials said. A small percentage of people with deportation orders — a few thousand a year — are not accepted back by their home countries, and under a 2001 Supreme Court ruling, they must be released from detention.

THE DEPARTURE POINT

Just as there are several possible outcomes for an immigration case, there are also different ways to deport unauthorized immigrants. A lot of it depends on location. Mexican nationals typically are flown to cities such as Phoenix, San Diego, and Brownsville, Tex. From there, they are driven across the border in vans or buses or, in some cases, they simply walk across a bridge. Vans can often be seen leaving ICE's building in central Phoenix, disappearing in the hubbub of a big city's traffic as they shuttle deportees on their way back to Mexico.

Citizens of other countries generally are taken to cities that are home to one of the 24 field offices run by the immigration agency's enforcement and removal operations. These cities include Seattle, Las Vegas and Boise, Idaho, in the West; Omaha, St. Paul and Kansas City, Mo., in the heartland; and Miami and Harrisburg, Pa., in the East. From there, deportees are flown to their final destinations.

THE JOURNEY

ICE has its own air transportation arm and uses a combination of commercial and charter flights to move detainees among American cities and from the United States to foreign countries. There are regularly scheduled charter flights to countries that have a large and steady number of deportees, such as El Salvador and Honduras. The agency also shuttles deportees on charter flights to Europe, Asia and Africa, though less frequently. Recently, one such flight carried deportees to Somalia, an ICE spokeswoman said.

Deportees are shackled by their wrists and ankles on charter flights and on commercial flights if they are being escorted. Not all of them are escorted; the decision is based on whether they have a history of violent crimes or are deemed dangerous to others. During the flight, wrist shackles come off only while the deportees eat or use the restroom.

THE COST OF REPATRIATION

The cost of these trips is borne entirely by American taxpayers. ICE pays on average $8,419 per flight hour for charter flights, regardless of how many people they carry.

Having too many empty seats on these flights, and too often, were among the points of criticism of in audit performed by the Homeland Security Department's Office of Inspector General in 2015. Another was the circuitous routes taken by at least some of the detainees. In 2013, one flew from Seattle to El Paso to Phoenix, back to Seattle and back to Phoenix before landing in Guatemala.

AFTER ARRIVAL

Immigrants generally arrive at their destinations carrying nothing beyond the clothes they are wearing. They have no laces on their shoes and no belts on their pants, because of fears those can be used in suicide attempts.

The responsibility of the United States government is not to get them to their final destinations. From a drop-off point — an airport, a bridge over the Rio Grande in Texas or an assigned gate in other land border crossings — deportees must figure out how to reunite with relatives there or connect with the families they may have left behind.

One early morning last year, I watched at least a dozen men emerge from a small Mexican government office in Nogales, just south of the border, where the men had checked in upon arrival. They were visibly confused.

One man approached a taxi driver and asked, "How much to drive me to San Luis Potosí?" — a state in the heart of the country. He had no money. The taxi driver directed him to a boulevard nearby and told him to follow it to a soup kitchen run by the Kino Border Initiative, a nonprofit group that feeds and clothes deportees newly arrived in a country they had chosen to leave.

Five years earlier, Maria Rodriguez, 40, walked past that same office. She had no money and no idea where to go when she was dropped off in Nogales after her deportation. (Ms. Rodriguez later re-entered the United States after petitioning for asylum, invoking the dangers of drug cartel violence in her home state, Guerrero, Mexico. But she currently does not have legal status.)

"I asked a person I didn't even know to lend me her phone so I could call my husband," Ms. Rodriguez recalled in an interview this week. Her husband, then a legal permanent United States resident and now a citizen, crossed the border to bring her some clothing and cash before returning home to their four children in Phoenix.

Is It Possible to Resist Deportation in Trump's America?

BY MARCELA VALDES | MAY 23, 2017

ON MONDAY, FEB. 6, two days before Guadalupe García Aguilar made headlines as the first person deported under President Donald Trump's new executive orders on immigration, she and her family drove to the modest stucco offices of Puente, an organization that represents undocumented immigrants. It was a postcard day: warm and dry, hovering around 70 degrees, the kind of winter afternoon that had long ago turned Phoenix into a magnet for American retirees and the younger, mostly Latin American immigrants who mulch their gardens and build their homes.

García Aguilar and her family — her husband and two children — squeezed together with four Puente staff members into the cramped little office that the group uses for private consultations. Carlos Garcia, Puente's executive director, had bought a fresh pack of cigarettes right before the talk; he needed nicotine to carry him through the discomfort of telling García Aguilar that she would almost certainly be deported on Wednesday. Until that moment, she and her family had not wanted to believe that the executive orders Trump signed on Jan. 25 had made her expulsion a priority. She had been living in the United States for 22 years, since she was 14 years old; she was the mother of two American citizens; she had missed being eligible for DACA by just a few months. Suddenly, none of that counted anymore.

García Aguilar's troubles with Immigration and Customs Enforcement (ICE) began in 2008, after police raided Golfland Sunsplash, the amusement park in Mesa, Ariz., where she worked. She spent three months in jail and three months in detention. (ICE booked her under the last name "García de Rayos.") In 2013, an immigration court ordered her removal. Yet under pressure from Puente, which ultimately filed a class-action lawsuit contending that Maricopa County's work-site raids were unconstitutional, ICE allowed García Aguilar (and dozens of others) to remain in Arizona under what is known as an order of supervision. ICE could stay her removal because the Obama administration's guidelines for the agency specified terrorists and violent criminals as priorities for deportation. But Trump's January orders effectively vacated those guidelines; one order specifically instructed that "aliens ordered removed from the United States are promptly removed." García Aguilar, who had a felony for using a fabricated Social Security number, was unlikely to be spared.

Orders of supervision are similar to parole; undocumented immigrants who have them must appear before ICE officers periodically for "check-ins." García Aguilar's next check-in was scheduled for Wednesday, Feb. 8. She had three options, Garcia explained. She could appear as usual and hope for the best. She could try to hide. Or she could put up a fight, either from a place of sanctuary or by appearing for her check-in amid media coverage that Puente would organize on her behalf. Whatever she decided, he said, she would be wise to spend Tuesday preparing for separation from her children.

The family was devastated. García Aguilar left the meeting red-faced with tears.

The next day a dozen activists gathered at Puente to strategize for García Aguilar's case. After reviewing the logistics for the usual public maneuvers — Facebook post, news release, online petition, sidewalk rally, Twitter hashtag, phone campaign — they debated the pros and cons of using civil disobedience. In the final years of the Obama administration, activists in Arizona had come to rely on "C.D.," as they called it, to make their dissatisfaction known. Puente members had blocked roads and chained themselves in front of the entrance to Phoenix's Fourth Avenue Jail. Yet Francisca Porchas, one of Puente's organizers, worried about setting an unrealistic precedent with its membership. "For Lupita we go cray-cray and then everyone expects that," she said. What would they do if Puente members wanted them to risk arrest every time one of them had a check-in?

Ernesto Lopez argued that they needed to take advantage of this rare opportunity. A week earlier, thousands of people had swarmed airports around the country to protest the executive order barring citizens from seven Muslim-majority nations. "There's been a lot of conversation about the ban, but for everything else it's dead," Lopez said. "Nobody is talking about people getting deported. In a couple of months, it won't be possible to get that media attention."

Garcia wasn't sure a rally for García Aguilar would work. "We're literally in survival mode," Garcia told me that week. It was too early to tell how ICE would behave under Trump, but they were braced for the worst. Nobody had a long-term plan yet. Even as he and his staff moved to organize the news conference, his mind kept running through the possibilities: Would it help García Aguilar stay with her family? Would it snowball into an airport-style protest? Would it cause ICE to double down on her deportation? He decided it was worth trying.

Shortly before noon on Wednesday, García Aguilar and her lawyer, Ray Ybarra Maldonado, entered ICE's field office as supporters chanted "No está sola!" (You are not alone!) behind her. Telemundo, Univision and ABC shot footage. Supporters posted their own videos on Twitter and Facebook. ICE security warily eyed the scene. An hour later, Ybarra Maldonado exited ICE alone. García Aguilar had been taken into custody. All around the tree-shaded patio adjacent to ICE's building, Puente members teared up, imagining the same dark future for themselves. Ybarra Maldonado filed a stay of deportation, and Porchas told everyone to come back later for a candlelight vigil.

That night a handful of protesters tried to block several vans as they sped from the building's side exit. More protesters came running from an ICE decoy bus that had initially distracted those attending the vigil out front. Manuel Saldaña, an Army veteran who did two tours in Afghanistan, planted himself on the ground next to one van's front tire, wrapping his arms and legs around the wheel. The driver looked incredulous; if he moved the van forward now, he would break one of Saldaña's legs. Peering through the van windows with cellphone flashlights, protesters found García Aguilar sitting in handcuffs. The crowd doubled in size. "Those shifty [expletive]," Ybarra Maldonado said as he stared at the van. ICE, he said, had never notified him that her stay of deportation had been denied.

Four hours later, García Aguilar was gone. After the Phoenix Police arrested seven people and dispersed the crowd, ICE took her to Nogales, Mexico. By then images of García Aguilar and the protest were already all over television and social media. She and her children became celebrities within the immigrant rights movement. Carlos Garcia, who was with her in Nogales, told me that Mexican officials stalked her hotel, hoping to snag a photo. "Everyone wanted to be the one to help her," he said. "Everyone wanted a piece." Later that month, her children — Jacqueline, 14, and Angel, 16 — sat in the audience of Trump's first address to Congress, guests of two Democratic representatives from Arizona, Raúl Grijalva and Ruben Gallego.

During the Obama years, most immigrant rights organizations focused on big, idealistic legislation: the Dream Act and comprehensive immigration reform, neither of which ever made it through Congress. But Puente kept its focus on front-line battles against police-ICE collaboration. For Garcia, who was undocumented until a stepfather adopted him at 16, the most important thing is simply to contest all deportations, without exception. He estimates that Puente has had a hand in stopping about 300 deportations in Arizona since 2012.

Ever since Arizona passed Senate Bill 1070, one of the toughest anti-undocumented bills ever signed into law, the state has been known for pioneering the kind of draconian tactics that the Trump administration is now turning into federal policy. But if Arizona has been a testing ground for the nativist agenda, it has also been an incubator for resistance to it. Among the state's many immigrant rights groups, Puente stands out as the most seasoned and most confrontational. In the weeks and months following Election Day 2016 — as progressive groups suddenly found themselves on defense, struggling to figure out how to handle America's new political landscape — Garcia was inundated with calls for advice. He flew around the country for training sessions with field organizers, strategy meetings with lawyers and policy experts and an off-the-record round table with Senators Dick Durbin and Bernie Sanders in Washington. A soft-spoken man with a stoic demeanor and a long, black ponytail, Garcia was also stunned by Trump's victory. But organizers in Phoenix had one clear advantage. "All the scary things that folks are talking about," he told me, "we've seen before." On Nov. 9, he likes to say, the country woke up in Arizona.

During the 1990s, after President Bill Clinton's administration cracked down on illegal entries at the border near San Diego, migrants crossed the desert into Arizona instead, and the state's undocumented population swelled. In response, the State Legislature passed laws intended to make the daily lives of the undocumented untenable, a legal strategy known as "attrition through enforcement." Arizona cut off access to driver's licenses, to social services, to in-state college tuition; it reclassified the use of a fake Social Security number to gain employment as a felony. In 2007 Maricopa County — an area that includes nearly four million people and the cities of Phoenix, Scottsdale and Mesa — went further, signing what's known as a 287(g) agreement with ICE. At the time, fewer than 70 police organizations in the country had 287(g)s, more than half of them in the Southeast. These agreements give local law-enforcement agencies the power to place immigration detainers inside jails and to assemble task forces to arrest people suspected of being undocumented while out on patrol.

That year Arizona's undocumented population reached roughly half a million people. In Maricopa County, Sheriff Joseph Arpaio aimed to make that number plummet. He directed police to conduct "crime suppression" sweeps in predominantly Latino neighborhoods and to raid businesses. During sweeps, police would often detain Latinos for minor offenses like honking a car horn, then demand proof of legal residence.

Maricopa County voters appeared delighted with his tactics; for a time, "Sheriff Joe" was the most popular elected official in the state. Support for him may have been abetted by Arizona's dismal economy.

Phoenix had been one of the centers of the building boom; in 2006, business owners in the state said they needed a Mexican guest-worker program to meet the demand for cheap manual labor. But in the spring of 2007, Arizona's housing market began to crater. In 2008, the state had 117,000 foreclosures, the third-highest number in the country.

For readers of Mexican-American history, this sudden hardening of attitudes toward the undocumented was unsurprising: America has long maintained a love-hate relationship with Spanish-speaking labor. During the Great Depression, at least one million Mexican nationals and Mexican-Americans were forcibly repatriated. The following decade, the United States began importing 4.6 million Mexicans to satisfy labor shortages in agricultural fields. But even as that program continued in the 1950s, President Eisenhower's administration sent another one million back to Mexico by truck, train and ship in a roundup known as "Operation Wetback."

Near Miami, Ariz., a young Alfredo Gutierrez and his family escaped capture by camping in the mountains. "One of the reasons they got away with repatriation and they got away with Wetback was because there was no resistance," Gutierrez, who later became an Arizona state senator, told me. "Everyone of that era will tell you how they hid." But when Arpaio came for the undocumented, many of them argued for their right to stay. This transformation was due, in great part, to Puente.

During its early years, Puente planned protest marches, organized boycotts against local businesses that supported Arpaio and ran know-your-rights classes in Spanish. When Arizona Republicans passed S.B.1070 in 2010, Puente and the National Day Laborer Organizing Network began a national boycott that was estimated to cost Arizona over $200 million in canceled business conferences; 100,000 people marched against the bill in Phoenix. T-shirts with the slogan "Legalize Arizona" popped up in places like Chicago and New York.

Yet these actions did little to stop actual deportations. So in the wake of S.B.1070, Puente adopted a new organizing strategy, setting up neighborhood defense committees, or comités del barrio, throughout Maricopa County. "We had to build a base," Garcia explains; five or six leaders planning actions in a room was no longer enough. Through the comités, Puente cultivated relationships with hundreds of undocumented people and their families with the goal of piecing together a detailed understanding of how ICE and Arpaio worked. By 2011, it could draw a map tracing the system from arrest to deportation — and mark each point along the way where a person had the possibility of release.

In comités, people learned several ways of avoiding deportation. If a police officer pulled them over while driving, they could exercise their constitutional right to remain silent when they were asked whether they were American citizens. If an officer didn't explicitly detain them, they could walk away from their cars to avoid further questions. If officers appeared at their homes, they could demand to see a warrant before opening the door. The comités also taught people how to argue their own cases if they were handed over to ICE. (Undocumented immigrants have no right to a public defender but often may plead their cases before an immigration judge.) Puente encouraged its members to hash out legal strategies with a lawyer before they ever were detained — and to sign a copy of a Department of Homeland Security form authorizing media interviews in detention. Because their weekly meetings built genuine social ties, the comités also helped mobilize rapid responses to deportation. Members were more likely to show up for one another at protest rallies.

But even as the comités were being assembled, there was lingering tension within the broader immigrant-activist community over whether "Dreamers," who had been brought to the United States as minors, should represent themselves separately from the rest of the undocumented population. Undocumented students at Arizona State University had organized themselves into their own tightly knit group, the Arizona Dream Act Coalition (ADAC). Nurtured by other organizers and inspired by the national organization United

We Dream, ADAC members came out of the shadows to push Congress to pass the Dream Act and to fight for other legislative exceptions, like in-state tuition. "Early on, a lot of Dreamers wouldn't even talk about deportations," Garcia says. "It was all about the Dream Act, figuring out tuition and those sorts of things, driver's licenses." He was irritated by the Dreamers' tendency to portray themselves as innocent victims, a tactic that opened the door for conservatives to speak of Dreamers with empathy even as they cracked down on their parents as "criminals." (Trump has expressed support for Dreamers.) "A lot us feel like we sort of shot ourselves in the foot," Erika Andiola, ADAC's first president, told me after Trump's election. "Because we started that narrative like 'I was brought here by my parents, not my fault, poor me, I was here as a child' that kind of created blame on our parents."

But after S.B.1070's "papers please" law overcame court battles and went into effect in September 2012 — three months after the Obama administration created Deferred Action for Childhood Arrivals (DACA) — collaborations between Puente and ADAC increased. In Arizona, the police were now obligated to question anyone that they had "reasonable suspicion" to believe was undocumented. As a result, a new wave of undocumented residents, including many Dreamers' parents, found themselves snared in deportation proceedings.

Andiola's own mother, Maria Guadalupe Arreola, was stopped while driving in Mesa in September 2012; the police passed her information along to ICE. Three months later, ICE agents appeared at the family's home and took Arreola away in handcuffs. Andiola responded by flipping open her laptop and filming a video that she posted to social media. Within hours of her mother's arrest, the hashtags #WeAreAndiola and #SomosAndiola were rousing people over Facebook and Twitter. ICE's office in Phoenix was flooded with calls. Messages also poured into the Department of Homeland Security from Washington; hours before ICE had banged on her door, Andiola was hired by an Arizona congresswoman, Kyrsten Sinema.

The next morning, as Arreola sat on a bus headed for Nogales, protesters rallied outside of ICE's Phoenix office, drawing television crews. The bus driver received a phone call. The bus turned around. A few hours later, Arreola was released with an order of supervision signed by ICE's field-office director, Katrina Kane. Jose Luis Peñalosa, the lawyer who represented Arreola at the time, believes the directive to reverse the deportation must have come directly from Washington.

Under Obama, Andiola told me, the primary strategy had been to create a well-publicized "moral dilemma" between Obama's pro-immigrant rhetoric and his aggressive immigration enforcement — exactly what she had done with her mother. Such dilemmas could provoke ICE to use prosecutorial discretion to stop a removal.

By 2014, however, such maneuvers rarely worked. After Obama won re-election and Democrats lost the midterms, Washington was less susceptible to public shaming. Phone campaigns and news conferences no longer resulted in release. "We got to a point where the legal strategy, the political strategy wasn't working," Andiola said, "so we had to begin using our bodies in civil disobedience." In August 2013, ADAC stopped an ICE bus full of deportees in Phoenix, delaying their removal. In 2014 Andiola and Garcia were arrested together during a hunger strike outside ICE's field office.

By then Andiola had left her leadership position at ADAC, whose board at that time disapproved of its members' involvement in non-Dreamer cases. She also abandoned the job as a congressional staffer, frustrated by the lack of movement on comprehensive immigration reform. When people facing deportation petitioned her for help, as scores did through Facebook, she sent them to Puente, which her own mother joined. "Puente and us were trying to do the same thing with parents," Andiola said. ADAC could no longer help them, but Puente would.

Late on the night of García Aguilar's protest, after the chants stopped and the crowd dwindled to a handful of private conversations, an ADAC veteran asked Andiola how she thought she might handle her own mother's check-in with ICE in May. "I don't know," Andiola snapped. "I don't know. I don't know." A few weeks later at a Puente meeting, when Porchas asked how she was doing, Andiola simply began crying. Andiola walked over the desert into Arizona with her mother in 1998, when she was 11, primarily to escape her father. He was an abusive alcoholic, she said, with a taste for firing guns indoors. He was still alive in Durango; Arreola was terrified of seeing him again.

But after what happened with García Aguilar, Andiola knew that the tactics she used to stave off her mother's deportation in 2013 would no longer work. "He's not going to listen," Andiola said of Trump. "He's not going to care." The week ICE deported García Aguilar, more than 600 undocumented immigrants were picked up in raids across the country. This in itself wasn't unusual: ICE surges had occurred many times during Obama's presidency, including, notoriously, over New Year's weekend 2016. Yet because Trump's presidential campaign had promised millions of deportations, the surge could now be spun as a change in federal policy. Trump himself basked in the news. "The crackdown on illegal criminals is merely the keeping of my campaign promise," he tweeted that Sunday. "Gang members, drug dealers & others are being removed!"

"We've always had these really broad laws so what the history really is about is what the executive wants to enforce," Hiroshi Motomura, a law professor at U.C.L.A., told me, recalling the Palmer Red Raids of 1919 and 1920 and the Japanese internment camps of the 1940s. "Right now, we see the swing of the pendulum back to the harshest possible interpretation." The velocity of this swing is possible because most of the victories achieved by the undocumented during Obama's administration depended upon the use of prosecutorial discretion.

Until the 1970s, immigration officials staunchly denied that they ever allowed any illegal immigrant to remain in the country with their approval. Prosecutorial discretion was exposed only after President Richard Nixon tried to throw John Lennon, the former Beatle, out of the country before the 1972 elections. (Nixon feared that Lennon, who opposed the war in Vietnam, might turn younger voters against him.)

In the course of defending Lennon — as the Penn State law professor Shoba Sivaprasad Wadhia details in her book, "Beyond Deportation" — his lawyer, Leon Wildes, unearthed a trove of documents proving the existence of a hidden "deferred action" program, which allowed immigration officials to use prosecutorial discretion to grant "nonpriority" status to individuals on humanitarian grounds. After Wildes spotlighted the program, he won deferred action for Lennon, allowing one of the world's most famous musicians to stay in the United States long enough to gain lawful permanent residence.

Until Obama came into office, gaining "deferred action" or "nonpriority" status required the help of a savvy immigration lawyer. "I used to call it the invisible sword," Wadhia told me, noting that, outside the DACA program, there has never been any official form to fill out or fee to pay in order to win deferred action. Obama did not invent prosecutorial discretion, but he did make it more transparent and accessible, standing in the Rose Garden to announce how his administration had used it to create a deferred-action program for Dreamers. Trump cannot destroy prosecutorial discretion — it's what allows a district attorney to ignore shoplifting so she can focus on murders — but his administration can pressure ICE officials to resist appeals to exercise it favorably.

And that's exactly what many believe has happened. In the past, when Washington-based officials pressured ICE supervisors to reverse decisions, as seems to have happened in Arreola's case, ICE agents had little recourse. Even immigration judges could find their orders for deportation halted by prosecutorial discretion, as in the case of García Aguilar. But those roadblocks have been undone. "Some 60,000 agents, they have been chafing at prosecutorial-discretion memos," Paromita Shah, the associate director of the National Immigration Project, told me in November.

In fact, García Aguilar's deportation was just the first of many cases in which undocumented residents who were granted nonpriority status found themselves deported when they appeared for routine check-ins. ICE now commonly instructs people to appear for check-ins with passports, which makes their deportation easier. With prosecutorial discretion held out of reach, Garcia told me, "once ICE decides to deport someone, it's nearly impossible to get them out of their grasp."

This is exactly the situation that Andiola feared when we met for coffee on a cold, drizzly day last November. Many of the cases that activists won under Obama, she said, weren't actually closed; they were merely suspended through prosecutorial discretion. "The judge says, 'I'm not saying I'm not going to deport you, but I'm going to put your file away and you can just stay,'" she said. "Those cases are easy to just open up again." In April, ICE officially reopened her own mother's file, sending Arreola a letter ordering her to report for removal at its Phoenix field office on May 3. "Everything's going to change for me, for my life," Arreola told me, weeping, the day after the letter arrived. "Ay, I don't want to cry, I don't want to cry, I don't want to cry."

On a blazing afternoon this May, signs lay stacked in piles throughout Puente's large meeting room. Blue hummingbirds on one sign flew through the words "Resist!" "¡Resiste!"; on another, Aztec gods pointed like Uncle Sam over the question "Who you calling illegal, Pilgrim?" Sitting at a plastic table amid the slogans, her hair braided in preparation for a long march through high heat, Maria Castro, an ADAC veteran who had become a Puente organizer, explained to me how Puente's strategy had shifted in the months since the effort to save García Aguilar failed. With a black crayon, she drew six boxes in a row, each symbolizing a stage in the deportation process: police, city court, prison, ICE, immigration court, deportation. Before Trump, she said, Puente had focused its efforts on stopping deportations at ICE or after. But now that Trump had vacated Obama's priorities and reduced the likelihood of prosecutorial discretion, "everything from city court forward no longer works." She drew a red line through five of the boxes, leaving only one unscathed: the initial point of police contact.

After Arpaio fully lost his 287(g) status in 2011 amid allegations of abuse, he allowed ICE to install an agent inside central booking at the Fourth Avenue Jail in Phoenix. Because that agent could question anyone charged with any offense right after fingerprinting, Castro told me, most undocumented people who are arrested in Maricopa County have an ICE hold on them by the time they are arraigned. Last year, ICE requested the detention of 3,483 people in Maricopa County jails. The signs lying around the room were for Puente's May Day march, the theme of which was "ICE out of Fourth Avenue."

Last fall many assumed that Trump would instigate huge round-ups of the undocumented, á la Operation Wetback. Yet so far, the process for deportations in Arizona has mostly followed the pattern set by Arpaio; the undocumented are first caught by the police. (Nationally, however, ICE's noncriminal arrests have increased 157 percent compared to the first four months of 2016.) "Trump doesn't have to do much to deport anyone he wants to because Obama has already built this machinery for him," Garcia told me. Under Obama, 287(g) agreements proliferated. In 2006, ICE was allocated $5 million to implement such agreements. A year into Obama's first term, that number shot up to $68 million, though it was reduced to $24 million in 2014.

Obama also beefed up ICE's power by expanding the Bush-era information-sharing network known as Secure Communities. In 2009, Secure Communities connected only 88 jurisdictions to ICE. By 2013, ICE was linked to every jurisdiction in the nation. What difference does such an expansion make? When Arreola was taken to a police station after her traffic stop in 2012, she refused to answer the questions. Are you a citizen of the United States? Do you have a Social Security number? Were you born in Mexico? But when her fingerprints were run through ICE's database, they got a hit. "Be nice," Arreola recalls one officer saying sarcastically in English, as he held up a piece of paper with her mug shot on it. The photo had been taken in 1998, after her first, failed attempted to enter the United States.

Obama deported nearly three million undocumented immigrants, more than any president in American history. For Puente, one of the stranger outcomes of Trump's election is that, for the first time, they stand a chance of dismantling some police-ICE collaborations.

Fighting individual deportation cases has become harder, but policy battles have gained traction in Phoenix, where Democrats still hold significant power. "Now it's convenient for Democrats to shame a deportation," Garcia told me.

Under Obama, he speculated, many Democrats were reluctant to oppose any of the president's policies. Under Trump, they saw political advantage in talking about deportations, sanctuary cities and immigrant rights — especially now that the undocumented had found new allies. When Garcia helped assemble the coalition United Against Hate after Trump's victory in November, 56 groups signed up. That same month, Paul Penzone defeated Joe Arpaio at the polls. For Garcia, who began his activism under President George W. Bush, one great lesson of the past eight years is that Democrats are unreliable allies, willing to place other policy goals, like the Affordable Care Act, above the needs of the undocumented. "Neither party is our friend," he said. But the two-party system, he knew, could be played to Puente's advantage as it pushed for Phoenix to do more cite-and-release actions instead of arrests and as it argued for school boards to reduce the number of police officers in schools.

None of these policy advances could save someone already facing deportation. That May Day, García Aguilar's family joined hundreds of protesters for Puente's march from Arizona's Capitol to the Fourth Avenue Jail. García Aguilar's daughter, Jacqueline, and Arreola spoke at the final rally. "With ICE there's now no right or wrong," García Aguilar's husband told me, as the crowd marched around the jail three times, losing more people with each turn. His wife had decided not to hide from ICE, he said, because living on the lam "no es vida." But as time goes by, he finds her absence more and more difficult. "Now," he said, "maybe it's better not to show up."

I heard anecdotal accounts that more people were, in fact, choosing the option that his wife had declined. Some were moving to new addresses. Others were looking for sanctuary in churches or simply shutting themselves up in their homes, essentially becoming fugitives when their check-ins passed. The full extent of these changes won't be clear until this summer, said Petra Falcon, the executive director of Promise Arizona (PAZ). During past crises in Arizona, she said, undocumented parents had often waited for classes to end before moving with their children. But a recent report from the Arizona Health Care Cost Containment System showed that the percentage of Hispanics participating in Arizona's state health care system had fallen by more than half between October 2016 and April 2017. Some Hispanics, it appeared, might be trying to retreat into the shadows again.

Trump's Jan. 25 orders have made the concept of a single national strategy to stop deportations irrelevant. Under Obama, ICE's prosecutorial priorities were consistent from state to state because they were clearly defined by the Department of Homeland Security and ICE in Washington. Trump's orders, however, expanded prosecutorial priorities so broadly that, as a practical matter, there no longer exist any priorities at all. Steve Legomsky, the former chief counsel of United States Citizenship and Immigration Services (U.S.C.I.S.), told me that, effectively, "the decision of what to prioritize is now left in the hands of each individual ICE agent and each individual C.B.P. border-patrol officer." Much has been made of the fact that Trump has essentially ceded America's military strategy to its generals. His handling of ICE, whose field directors now set the agency's direction, appears similar.

Legomsky said that the sweep of Trump's priorities has also given ICE cover for the use of targeted deportations against activists. The agency doesn't need to explain why the deportation of a DACA activist or an undocumented organizer is consistent with their announced priorities, he said, "if the announced priorities cover almost everybody." In February, the Department of Homeland Security seemed to give its blessing for such retaliations when it issued a memo that gave ICE officers the authority to prioritize the deportation of anyone they believed posed "a risk to public safety." Andiola, who is now the political director of Our Revolution, the 501(c)(4) that sprang from Bernie Sanders's presidential bid, didn't know if her mother had been targeted or if the letter ordering her to report for removal was simply a consequence of Trump's redefined priorities.

After Arreola received the letter, Andiola worked her extensive professional network, calling organizers, lawyers and activists to gather opinions about what she should do. "It's great that there are so many perspectives," she said, "but it's difficult to sort through all the differing kinds of advice." Eventually, she realized there was no single solution. With a diversity of tactics in her pocket, she would deploy one after another in hopes of reaching success. What she needed first, she decided, was a legal strategy.

Even though Arreola fled to the United States to escape domestic abuse, it never occurred to either woman that Arreola might be eligible for asylum. In Andiola's mind, asylum seekers came from Central America or the Middle East, places with extreme political turmoil. After García Aguilar's deportation, though, Andiola began to take the option seriously. She knew it was a long shot: It has never been easy for Mexicans to gain asylum in the United States. And though several lawyers told me that asylum applications are now rising, the process is likely to become even more difficult soon. The Jan. 25 order on border security includes an entire section declaring Trump's intention "to end the abuse of parole and asylum provisions." "It's the same political agenda that is behind banning Muslims and refugees from coming to the U.S.," says Marielena Hincapié, the executive director of the National Immigration Law Center.

A successful asylum application, Andiola learned, depended upon documentary evidence. Arreola recalled that a newspaper in Durango once published her ex-partner's photograph, noting that he had been charged for the kidnapping and rape of a minor: her. In Durango, Arreola's brother-in-law found a copy of a 1991 police report detailing one of her ex-partner's rages. These two documents formed the backbone of the asylum application Arreola used to request an interview with U.S.C.I.S. in April. Within a week, she had an appointment for a "reasonable fear" interview to determine if her case merited serious consideration. Three days after the interview, Arreola received good news: ICE had canceled her scheduled removal on May 3. She had passed the interview, the first of many steps in gaining asylum. Her lawyer, Ray Ybarra Maldonado, who also represents García Aguilar, says there is still a fair chance that Arreola's application for asylum may be denied, but she was now safe to report for her check-in on May 23.

On May 3, the day Arreola was to have been deported, Arreola and Andiola gathered with friends, family and supporters for a prayer breakfast at the First Congregational United Church of Christ in Phoenix, which had offered to house Arreola if she chose sanctuary. Pastor James Pennington had been active in the fight for gay rights. The patio of First Congregational was decorated with several flags, including a rainbow flag, an Arizona state flag and an American flag. Inside the church, members of Puente and former members of ADAC formed a circle with several non-Hispanics who had only recently allied themselves with the undocumented. Standing together they recited Psalm 30 in Spanish:

> *Te ensalzaré, oh Señor, porque me has elevado, y no has permitido que mis enemigos se rían de mi.*

> *I'll praise you, Lord, because you've lifted me up. You haven't let my enemies laugh at me.*

Yet their enemies remained hard at work. A week later, Marco Tulio Coss Ponce, who had been living in Arizona under an order of supervision since 2013, appeared at ICE's field office in Phoenix with his lawyer, Ravindar Arora, for a check-in. ICE officers, Arora said, knew that Coss Ponce was about to file an application for asylum — several of his relatives had been recently killed or threatened by the Sinaloa cartel in Mexico — and they had assured Arora several times that Coss Ponce would not be removed. They said he simply needed to wear an ankle monitor to make sure he didn't disappear. The fitting was delayed several times until finally Arora had to leave to argue a case in court. After he departed, ICE officers handcuffed Coss Ponce and put him in a van, alone. Three hours later, he was in Nogales.

In a 'Sanctuary City,' Immigrants Are Still at Risk

BY LIZ ROBBINS | FEB. 27, 2018

FROM THE EARLY DAYS of the Trump administration, Mayor Bill de Blasio proclaimed that he would defend the residents of New York from the newly aggressive immigration authorities, "regardless of where they come from, regardless of their immigration status."

A year later, the federal government has ratcheted up its attacks against so-called sanctuary cities like New York — including Chicago, Philadelphia and San Francisco — threatening to withhold millions of dollars in federal funding for law enforcement programs and detaining growing numbers of undocumented residents. Cities faced a Friday deadline to prove their cooperation with the immigration authorities, as the United States Immigration and Customs Enforcement agency, known as ICE, continued making arrests. Nationwide, the number of arrests in 2017 increased 41 percent from the year before.

In New York, where some 500,000 residents are undocumented, if ICE wants to arrest somebody, it can. "Putting a bubble over a city where ICE can't penetrate is not possible," said Camille Mackler, the legal policy director of the New York Immigration Coalition, an activist group. "People think 'sanctuary city' — that you're able to walk freely without fear. That's not the case."

ICE agents have been appearing in New York's courthouses and at people's front doors, and, according to immigrant advocates, even entered a Manhattan church with a Spanish-speaking immigrant congregation. While the New York Police Department does not generally hand over detainees to ICE, it does, through a bureaucratic backdoor, essentially provide a road map: Arrest information is sent to the state, which shares it with the Federal Bureau of Investigation. ICE can now see that information.

Federal agents recently arrested an undocumented immigrant from Ivory Coast as he left Bronx Criminal Court, part of stepped-up enforcement by the Trump administration.

"It's hardly a sanctuary," said Muzaffar Chishti, the director of the Migration Policy Institute's office at New York University School of Law. "The mayor of the City of New York does not hide people under his desk. We're fully cooperating with ICE. People get deported from New York all the time."

Immigration arrests of residents without criminal records more than tripled in New York after President Trump took office. Of the 2,976 arrests in 2017, 899 were of people without criminal convictions, up from 250 out of 1,762 in 2016, according to ICE statistics. Under the Obama administration, undocumented immigrants without criminal records were not priorities for deportation.

Mr. de Blasio often says that the term "sanctuary city" is misinterpreted: It is a policy intended to make undocumented victims or witnesses feel safe to report crimes to the police without fear of immigration repercussions.

To that end, New York does not deputize police officers to carry out immigration laws, under a policy known as 287g, which Mr. Trump has strongly supported. Since 2014, the city has declined to honor what are known as detainers — requests by ICE to hold undocumented immigrants who have been charged or convicted of crimes for 48 hours past their release dates so that immigration agents can pick them up. The city also removed immigration authorities from the Rikers Island jail complex where they had easy access to prisoners when they were released. "It forces them to go to inconvenient and costly routes to get to their target," Mr. Chishti said.

New York's detainer law, however, has exceptions: The police must turn over a person convicted of one of 170 serious crimes within the last five years — including arson, homicide, rape or robbery — and in cases in which a judge has signed a detainer request.

ICE issued 1,526 detainer requests to the New York Police Department in the 2017 fiscal year, up from 80 in 2016. The Police Department complied with none of them.

By its own policy, ICE does not enter places of worship, schools and hospitals. But courthouses have become frequent sites of arrests because they offer a degree of control that agents would not have when going to people's homes. "Because courthouse visitors are typically screened upon entry to search for weapons and other contraband, the safety risks for the arresting officers and for the arrestee inside such a facility are substantially diminished," ICE said in a statement.

According to the Immigrant Defense Project, a nonprofit organization that is tracking arrests at city and state courthouses, 87 arrests were made in New York City courts in 2017, compared with six in 2016. So far, this year, there have been 13 courthouse arrests.

Aboubacar Dembele, 27, was one. He was surrounded by immigration agents moments after stepping out of a hearing in Bronx Criminal Court. Mr. Dembele, an undocumented immigrant from the Ivory Coast, had pleaded not guilty to an assault charge stemming from a fight on a city bus in December; the judge had reduced the charge to

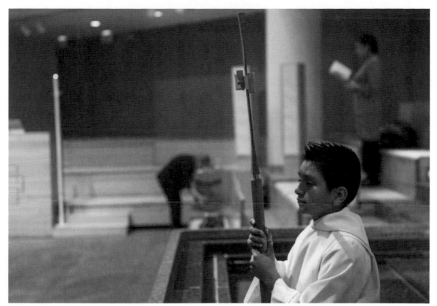

The Iglesia de Sion at Saint Peter's Lutheran Church in Midtown Manhattan has a predominantly Hispanic congregation. A pastor there said immigration agents showed up in the lobby of the church, and he escorted them out.

a misdemeanor from a felony, and had set a follow-up court date to address the charges. Instead, Mr. Dembele is awaiting deportation at the Hudson County Correctional Facility in Kearny, N.J. "The way that they come and ambush people is outrageous," said his lawyer, Monica Dula, of the Legal Aid Society of New York.

Mr. Dembele was placed on ICE's radar because of his arrest; his court appearance was public record. In January, ICE clarified its policy to say that it would not arrest family members or witnesses. Actions inside courthouses, it said, would be against "targeted aliens with criminal convictions, gang members, national security or public safety threats."

"The public is led to believe that ICE is pulling out dangerous individuals," the Brooklyn district attorney, Eric Gonzalez, said at a news conference to denounce ICE's courthouse actions. He added that low-level offenders are more often being arrested. "There is a chilling effect on our noncitizen and immigrant populations."

As he spoke, ICE agents were in a Brooklyn courthouse to pick up a defendant. The judge postponed the case when the man's lawyer, Roger Asmar, told her that his client was afraid to appear.

Mr. Gonzalez has instructed prosecutors to bring lesser charges against immigrants accused of low-level offenses so as not to trigger deportations or affect their immigration applications, and the Manhattan district attorney, Cyrus R. Vance Jr., has declined to prosecute most people arrested for evading the fare on the subways. Mr. de Blasio has come out against that idea, however, for public-safety reasons.

The city, which has provided a municipal ID card often used by undocumented residents, has also allocated $47.5 million for immigrant legal services this year.

To the ire of some immigrant activists, Mr. de Blasio said the money could not be used to aid undocumented immigrants convicted of the serious crimes defined by the detainer law. The New York City Bar Association wrote him a letter claiming "it was fundamentally unfair" to deny people legal help, including those eligible for a complex form of relief for victims of domestic violence or unaccompanied minors.

Last summer, Mr. de Blasio eliminated city money for that same class of immigrants in deportation proceedings. The City Council secured private funding to keep representing clients who fell into this category.

At times, it seems that Mr. de Blasio's fierce rhetoric has given some immigrants an inflated sense of security. In December, two ICE officers entered the downstairs lobby of Saint Peter's Church in Midtown Manhattan that houses a Spanish-speaking congregation, La Iglesia de Sion, according to the Rev. Amandus J. Derr, a pastor at Saint Peter's. Father Derr escorted the two men from the building. An official for ICE said it could not confirm that the officers were from the enforcement agency.

The incident left the congregation rattled and its numbers depleted. One member attending a recent Sunday Mass, Angela Carvajal, 49, relayed her fears. "I hope the mayor will do something about this," she said in Spanish. Her friend, Alicia Garcia-Fuentes, 40, added, "Isn't he supposed to protect the undocumented?"

The Americans Left Behind by Deportation

OPINION | BY KARLA CORNEJO VILLAVICENCIO | FEB. 28, 2018

IN THE FALL, I traveled to rural Ohio to meet with the children of a man who had been recently deported to Mexico, even though he was considered a model citizen by his neighbors and had no criminal record beyond driving without a license. I had seen video footage of his three young boys and little girl saying goodbye to him at the airport. They looked like orphaned bear cubs, wandering around aimlessly in the terminal, their faces frozen in fear.

Eric, the oldest at 14, is in the eighth grade and wants the local Wendy's to make an exception to its minimum age requirement so he can work there. "I'm the man of the house now," he told me. When their father left, so did the only member of the family who could drive. Eric walks several miles to the grocery store and returns carrying heavy bags of food even in the snow. Their mother, who is also undocumented, is now the family's sole source of income and works long hours at a factory, so Eric has to come straight home from school to take care of his younger siblings. (He had to scrap plans to try out for the wrestling team.)

Edwin, 12, has nightmares about his father and crawls into his mother's bed almost every night. Classmates taunt him that they hope his mother gets deported, too. Anuar, 10, who calms himself by doing equations in his head, brought me his report card with a perfect 100 in math. Elsiy, 6, has not been eating well since her father's been gone.

America's historic uneasiness with interracial marriage and mixed-race children has found a new incarnation in the persecution of families with mixed legal status. There are nearly six million citizen children who live with at least one undocumented parent, and perhaps millions of other Americans who are married to undocumented immigrants. Reports are multiplying of Immigration and Customs Enforcement agents picking up immigrants at their green card couple interviews, while their American spouses are left speechless and powerless. The Trump administration's aggressive detention and removal of undocumented immigrants is not only inhumane in its treatment of immigrants, but a direct attack on the rights and well-being of their American family members.

I recently met Jim Chuquirima, a 16-year-old American citizen whose mother is undocumented. He is bespectacled, painfully shy and builds computers out of spare parts that his mother, Nelly Cumbicos, buys him. Ms. Cumbicos is a movie-star-beautiful single mother from Ecuador who had sworn off men before she met Ramón Muñiz, a roofer and die-hard union man who lived on the first floor of the multifamily home in Meriden, Conn., where Jim and Nelly rented the third floor. He would fix Nelly's car, pick Jim up from school while she was at work and leave unsigned love letters on the windshield of her car.

They married in their home on Halloween in 2015. An American citizen, he insisted in 2015 that she let him petition for her green card, even though she was afraid it would put ICE on her trail. She was right: When ICE became aware of Ms. Cumbico's whereabouts, it located a deportation order from more than a decade before that she says she had never received because it was sent to a wrong address. ICE gave her a temporary stay on Feb. 5 only to inexplicably rescind it four days later. Like a botched execution, it left the family newly traumatized. Their legal fees have nearly bankrupted them. Her deportation is set for Wednesday.

"I feel like this is my fault," Mr. Muñiz said. "I put her in danger, but all I wanted was to protect her. I'm lost without her."

In the early 1900s, American women who married foreigners lost their citizenship. Those laws are off the books now. But does that mean American citizens have the constitutional right to be protected from the deportation of an immediate family member? Lower courts haven't thought so. In one case, the United States Court of Appeals for the Third Circuit decided the deportation of an American-born infant's parents didn't violate her right to grow up in this country because either her parents could surrender her to foster care in America before they left or she could leave with them and return to the United States as an adult. The Court of Appeals for the 10th Circuit has declared that a parent's deportation has only "incidental impact" on a child. Studies, however, have shown that children with parents who are under threat of deportation or have been deported fall into depression and anxiety and are more likely to have behavioral problems and to experience drastically decreased academic performance. Couples who are separated by oceans are very likely to end up divorced.

The Supreme Court has historically declared that it is "intolerable" to force a citizen to choose between two constitutional rights. But what then of the American families of deportees? Isn't the Trump administration forcing them to make a terrible choice, between either staying in the United States and having their families rived in two, or forfeiting their lives in America so that they can keep their families intact?

I, too, had to worry about this dilemma. I am the child of undocumented immigrants from Ecuador who brought me to this country when I was 5. I am the American dream incarnate, with an Ivy League education and a book deal. Now I am married to an American citizen, but there is no guarantee that my spouse's status will shield me from deportation.

For my own green card interview, I wore the collared pink silk J. Crew dress I wore to our wedding. I dress glamorously and wear a face full of designer makeup in any situation where I might be detained, out of pride and defiance. But this interview was not bait to detain me, the way interviews have been for so many less fortunate immigrants.

"There is nothing I wanted more than to be able to protect you from your nightmares," my partner told me after we'd read about the tragedy that had befallen other citizen-undocumented couples. "I wasn't thinking so much about the literal, legal rights that the green card would afford; I was thinking about what do I need to do to keep my family safe, and that meant making sure we could be a family. It was such a low bar."

I got my green card. Our marriage is real. My guilt is as well. It is so hard to imagine that Ramón's desire to keep Nelly safe provoked the exact opposite result.

Short of comprehensive immigration reform, which seems so unlikely these days, there are ways to end these inhumane deportations. In February 2017, John Kelly, then the secretary of homeland security, issued a memo essentially doing away with enforcement priorities for ICE, which generally called for not targeting undocumented immigrants if they did not have serious criminal records. The Kelly memo made all undocumented immigrants targets — even if they had spotless records, and even if they had spouses or children who were citizens. A return to Obama-era priorities that focused on criminals and security risks would restore some level of compassion to enforcement in the short term. Though far from the best solution, that would at least protect the rights of citizens.

Unless protecting American citizens was never the point of any of this.

KARLA CORNEJO VILLAVICENCIO is a graduate student in American studies at Yale.

Manhattan Church Shields Guatemalan Woman From Deportation

BY SHARON OTTERMAN | MARCH 28, 2018

AT THE END of a recent Sunday service, the congregants at the Fourth Universalist Society on Central Park West placed their hands on the shoulders of a woman who stood in the center of the church. Then other members reached forward to touch those people's shoulders, until the entire congregation was linked by touch like a radiating star.

It was a symbol of their commitment to put the woman, Aura Hernandez, 37, an undocumented Guatemalan immigrant, at the center of their church's life for what may be months or even years to come. Two weeks ago, Ms. Hernandez moved into a worn former office at the historic Upper West Side church with her 15-month-old daughter, Camila, to avoid deportation to Guatemala. In doing so, she joins about 40 other immigrants around the nation who are being publicly shielded by houses of worship. She vows to remain there, without going outside, until her immigration status changes.

"I don't intend to stand here with my arms crossed, and do nothing," Ms. Hernandez said in Spanish at the church on Tuesday, about her goal in seeking sanctuary. "I have to stand up and raise my voice because an injustice is being committed to me and to us. I think I'm here for a reason."

With help from other houses of worship and volunteers, this 130-member congregation will feed Ms. Hernandez, do the family's laundry, and help care for Camila, who is a U.S. citizen and can go outside. They will buy new carpet and paint for her room, and welcome Ms. Hernandez's 10-year-old son, Daniel, to live there on weekends and when the school year ends.

Daniel, also born in the United States, is living in Westchester County with Ms. Hernandez's husband, who also is undocumented.

It is a difficult situation, but the members of the Fourth Universalist, who met Ms. Hernandez at the March 18 service, said they

The congregants at the Fourth Universalist Society in Manhattan place their hands on the shoulders of Aura Hernandez, an undocumented Guatemalan immigrant, as a symbol of their commitment to put the woman at the center of their church's life.

were excited about being asked for help. Their Unitarian Universalist denomination calls for the use of social action to advance progressive principles, they explained. So for them, this is a unique opportunity.

"We call this room where we worship a sanctuary, and it has a brand new meaning right now," the Rev. Schuyler Vogel said at the service. "It has these stone walls, and they aren't just representational anymore. They protect actual people, keeping someone safe, to ensure that hate is kept out and love is held in."

Ms. Hernandez is the second person in New York City to publicly seek sanctuary in a church. The first, Amanda Morales Guerra, who is also from Guatemala, has been living in the Holyrood Episcopal Church in Washington Heights since August with her children, ages 10, 8 and 3.

Churches can effectively shield immigrants from deportation because houses of worship are considered sensitive sites where enforcement is avoided by the Immigration of Customs and Enforcement, commonly referred to as ICE. But ICE reserves the right to go into sensitive sites "in limited circumstances," according to its official policy.

As the weeks fold into months, living in a church takes a toll, both on the person and the church that is housing them. Stuck almost completely inside for nearly eight months, Ms. Morales said Wednesday she was experiencing panic attacks. "I had a dream this week that I was being strangled," she said in Spanish. "I was screaming and no one could hear me."

Ms. Hernandez makes tortillas in the church kitchen for Camila and cooks beans. There is a steady stream of visitors from immigrant organizations and the congregation. But at night, when the Gothic 19th-century building is quiet and dark, even going down the stairs to the bathroom can be terrifying, she said.

She cried when she talked about the happy life she had been leading, a difficult life of cleaning houses, but also the Sunday celebrations at the park, and her pride in her son's progress at school. In Guatemala, an abusive former partner has vowed to kill her, she said, and she has lost family members to violence.

These days, her son is a puddle of tears after his weekly visit. "I have to recover it," she said of her American life. "I owe it to my children."

While many undocumented immigrants are receiving legal help and other assistance, seeking church sanctuary remains a rarity, because of the toll it takes on families.

The idea behind the strategy is to give immigrants time to file legal appeals, while placing public pressure on ICE to grant reprieves, said Noel Andersen, of the Church World Service, an ecumenical human rights and refugee resettlement organization.

The strategy can work. Of the 39 immigrants who sought public sanctuary nationally in 2017, nine were granted reprieves from deportation, according to a database kept by the organization. Of the 12 who have sought sanctuary in 2018, six have gotten reprieves.

Not counted in those numbers are people who seek sanctuary in houses of worship without going public. In New York, about a dozen

Ms. Hernandez making tortillas for Camila in the church kitchen.

immigrants are hiding that way, according to Juan Carlos Ruiz of the New Sanctuary Coalition, which organizes sanctuary.

Each immigrant's case is unique, though a fear of violence if deported is a common theme, as is a desire to keep families together. Ms. Hernandez was 24 in 2005 when she crossed the border into Texas with a 9-year-old nephew. She was picked up by the Border Patrol within minutes of entering a town. During the three days of detention that followed, she alleges she was sexually abused by a border patrol officer. At the end of the third day, she said, another officer released her and her nephew and brought them to a bus stop, handing her some papers. "Welcome to the United States," she said the officer told her.

Traumatized, she said she never read the paperwork, which was in English. When she arrived at her sister's apartment in New York, she put it into a drawer. With time, and talking to a psychologist, she said she began to recover, getting a job and meeting her husband, who was from Mexico.

Then in 2013, she was caught in Mamaroneck, N.Y., driving the wrong way down a street that is one-way on Sundays. The police officer, seeing she had no documents, reported her to immigration officials. It was then she learned she had an active deportation order for failing to appear at a 2005 court date in Texas, she said.

A lawyer helped her file for a special visa available to crime victims after she told him about the sexual assault. But she said the appeal was ultimately denied, with immigration officials saying too many years had passed.

The New Sanctuary Coalition is seeking to reopen her case because of the assault allegation and the violence she says she would face in Guatemala. ICE officials did not respond to requests for comment. On Thursday, the New Sanctuary Coalition will announce Ms. Hernandez's presence in sanctuary at an event that will include a march around Trump International Hotel and Tower that will end at the church.

Ms. Hernandez said she hopes she will only have to be in the church for a few months, but she knows it may be longer. She does not see another way. "They abused me physically, psychologically, and now they want to separate me from my kids," she said in her makeshift quarters, sounding alternately despondent and defiant. "And that I will not stand for."

A Marriage Used to Prevent Deportation. Not Anymore.

BY VIVIAN YEE | APRIL 19, 2018

THEY HAD SHOWN the immigration officer their proof — the eight years of Facebook photos, their 5-year-old son's birth certificate, the letters from relatives and friends affirming their commitment — and now they were so close, Karah de Oliveira thought, so nearly a normal couple.

Thirteen years after her husband was ordered deported back to his native Brazil, the official recognition of their marriage would bring him within a few signatures of being able to call himself an American. With legal papers, they could buy a house and get a bank loan. He could board a plane. They could take their son to Disney World. Then the officer reappeared.

"I've got some good news and some bad news," he said. "The good

Leandro Arriaga with his wife, Katherine, and 15-month-old daughter, Jade. Mr. Arriaga came to the United States in 2001.

news is, I'm going to approve your application. Clearly, your marriage is real. The bad news is, ICE is here, and they want to speak with you."

ICE was Immigration and Customs Enforcement, the federal agency charged with arresting and deporting unauthorized immigrants — including, for the moment, Fabiano de Oliveira. In a back room of the immigration office in Lawrence, Mass., two agents were waiting with handcuffs. Her husband was apologizing, saying he was sorry for putting her through all of this.

Ms. de Oliveira kissed him goodbye. "I'll do whatever I can to get you out," she said.

For decades, marriage to a United States citizen has been a virtual guarantee of legal residency, the main hurdle being proof that the relationship is legitimate. But with the Trump administration in fierce pursuit of unauthorized immigrants across the country, many who were ordered deported years ago are finding that jobs, home and family are no longer a defense — not even for those who have married Americans.

As the Trump administration arrests thousands of immigrants with no criminal history and reshapes the prospects of even legal immigrants — an overdue corrective, officials say, to the lenient policies of the past — many who have lived without papers for years are urgently seeking legal status by way of a parent, adult child or spouse who is already a citizen or permanent resident.

In a growing number of cases, however, immigrants with old deportation orders that were never enforced are getting the go-ahead after an interview by United States Citizenship and Immigration Services, the agency that handles residency and citizenship, only to be arrested by ICE.

"It's like playing dice in Las Vegas or something," said William Joyce, a former immigration judge who now practices immigration law in Boston. "It's not 100 percent, but you're playing with fire if you go to that interview. You can walk in, but you won't be walking out."

Mr. de Oliveira and his wife had been dating for eight years, ever since Ms. de Oliveira's sister introduced them and they started working next door to each other — he at a pizza place, she at a Dunkin'

Donuts. They had a son three years later, but he waited until 2016 to marry Ms. de Oliveira, a Massachusetts native, partly because he did not want her family to think he was angling for a green card.

After the wedding, all the things they could not do while he lacked legal status became obvious: Not being able to go on their honeymoon, because he could not fly. Not being able to get a joint credit card. Not being able to get car insurance. "He got caught because he was trying to do the right thing," Ms. de Oliveira said of her husband's arrest on Jan. 9. "It was like a setup."

It took a month for her husband to be released. Because she did not know what else to say when their son asked, Ms. de Oliveira told him that his father was working out of town.

Like many of the immigrants detained this way, Mr. de Oliveira, a house painter, had no criminal history. To the Trump administration, the other thing they had in common was more germane: a legal but, until now, unenforced obligation to leave the country that had stuck to them for years, even as they pieced together lives and families in the United States.

In the later years of the Obama administration, the government mostly left people without criminal records alone, focusing instead on immigrants who had only recently arrived or had been convicted of serious crimes.

But the Trump administration emphasizes that everyone living here illegally is fair game for deportation, a policy that has bumped up immigration arrests by more than 40 percent since the beginning of 2017. Those who were ordered out of the country years ago are especially easy marks for an agency with limited resources for enforcement — especially if they walk straight into an immigration office.

ICE agents who once allowed many unauthorized immigrants to stay in the country as long as they checked in regularly have, over the past year, begun arresting many of those same immigrants at their once-routine ICE appointments. Unlike people who have had no prior contact with the immigration system, those who have already received orders of deportation have few, if any, protections against swift deportation.

Most who have been arrested under the Trump administration's policies had scant prospects of ever achieving legal status, whether through marriage to a citizen or another route. People like Mr. de Oliveira, on the other hand, were well on their way.

Getting a green card through spouses and relatives had become far easier in recent years for those who were living in the country illegally. Until 2013, undocumented applicants had to leave the country and wait out the application process from abroad, in some cases for as long as a decade, before returning with green cards.

Then the Obama administration created a waiver to abbreviate the process. Hurdles remained: Applicants still had to undergo vetting and security checks, for example, and prove that being deported would cause an American citizen — a spouse, for example — significant hardship. But once an immigration officer certified that their marriages were real, those with old deportation orders could ask an immigration judge to lift them so they could move on with their applications.

Now, however, it is risky simply to show up for an interview.

"For many individuals, it's sort of this Sophie's choice of remaining in the shadows, without formal immigration status," or hazarding arrest, said Genia Blaser, a staff attorney at the Immigrant Defense Project, a New York-based group that has been fielding calls from immigrants concerned about the new policies.

One such case made national headlines in the fall, when a Mexican man from the Denver area who had tried to obtain a green card through his daughter, a senior at Yale, was arrested at his residency interview. Despite a national campaign to get him released, the man, Melecio Andazola Morales, was deported in December.

On Feb. 8, immigration agents in San Francisco went a step further, arresting a Sudanese man at his interview for asylum, where he was supposed to be given a chance to explain why he feared returning to his home country. He had overstayed his visa, according to his lawyer, but had no criminal history or deportation order.

Immigration lawyers in New England, in particular, say there has been an unmistakable swell in the number of clients arrested at marriage interviews over the past few months. In the past, they said, U.S.C.I.S. officers had routinely alerted their counterparts at ICE to marriage applicants with old deportation orders, but only since President Trump took office had immigration agents begun to arrest those people at interviews. (A few such cases had occurred under the Bush administration as well, they said.)

Several lawyers said that they could no longer in good conscience encourage their clients to go to their marriage interviews, even if staying away would mean throttling a process that had already swallowed up months, if not years, and perhaps thousands of dollars in legal and application fees.

"So you end up with a situation where, all right, you don't go to the interview, you don't get the petition approved, so there's no way forward," said Mr. Joyce, who said at least five clients of his firm had been arrested in the middle of applying for a marriage-based green card over the last year, including two who were later deported.

An ICE spokesman, John Mohan, said that ICE has always worked with other government agencies to gather information for enforcement purposes. "ICE does not exempt classes or categories of removable aliens from potential enforcement," he said. "Any individual determined to be in violation of U.S. immigration laws may be subject to arrest, detention and removal from the United States."

Some remain undeterred. Leandro Arriaga, 43, had been warned by his lawyer that he might be detained at his marriage interview because he had been ordered deported years ago. But he decided to go anyway, determined to get legal papers. Without them, "You can't do nothing, you can't go to college, you can't do things in your own name," Mr. Arriaga said. "I said, 'I don't want to be illegal anymore. I've got to do something.' "

Mr. Arriaga had arrived illegally from the Dominican Republic in 2001, settling in the Boston area. He married a citizen, had three children, divorced, married another citizen and had another child, building a good business buying and fixing up old properties along the way.

After talking it over with his wife, Katherine, he decided to take a chance on the marriage interview, which was scheduled for March 2017 at the immigration office in Lawrence, Mass. An immigration officer certified his marriage, clearing him to move to the next step toward legalization. But before he could leave the office, he was detained, along with four other marriage applicants who were interviewing that morning, at least two of whom also had their petitions approved that morning.

It took until the end of May for him to get out of detention — more than two months of legal motions, court hearings and negotiations. The government ultimately released him with an ankle monitor, leaving Mr. Arriaga free to continue pursuing his application for a green card. Nearly a year later, though he was still chasing paperwork, he did not regret having walked into the immigration office. "I really think that I did the right thing," he said.

Many people, though, are heeding their lawyers' advice and postponing any application for legalization — even those who are likely to be deemed eligible. The risks are too great.

Natalia and Junior Roveda, who have been together seven years, managed to make it through their marriage interview last year in Massachusetts without incident. Mr. Roveda had come to the United States illegally from Brazil in 2005 and evaded a subsequent deportation order. He was moving into the next stage of the legalization process when he was arrested outside their apartment in the town of Framingham. In November, he was deported to Brazil, where he is now living with his parents.

Since then, his marble and granite business has gone dormant. Ms. Roveda, 25, gave up their apartment, sold the furniture and started working 20 extra hours a week at her job as an aesthetician and makeup artist to help support him in Brazil. When she can, she makes the long journey to visit him.

Still, Mr. Roveda is pursuing his green card from abroad. Their lawyers have told them it could take up to a year, and Mr. Roveda fears being stuck there, away from his wife and his faltering business, for much longer.

"It is not fair," he said. "I was already approved and everything."

Immigrants Claim Lawyers Defrauded Them and They May Be Deported

BY LIZ ROBBINS | MAY 3, 2018

AT THE TIME, Martin Torres Reyes thought he had found a path to a green card. It was early 2015, and Mr. Torres, an undocumented immigrant from Mexico, heard about a lawyer who was promising legal permanent residency to people who had lived in the United States for 10 years and had American-born children.

Mr. Torres went to see the lawyer, Thomas T. Hecht, at his Times Square office, and for an initial fee of $750, the lawyer said that he would get a work permit in six months, and then some time later, the green card.

According to a lawsuit filed late Wednesday in Federal District Court in Manhattan, this was fraud. Mr. Hecht and his son, Leonard H. Hecht, the complaint said, tricked Mr. Reyes and at least 25 other undocumented immigrants from New York.

The plaintiffs all thought they were applying for a green card, but instead, they claimed in the suit that the lawyers filed different paperwork, for asylum, without their knowledge.

"Our community is under attack from all directions, and they know it," Mr. Torres, 40, said in Spanish in an interview this week, referring to immigration lawyers. He paid a total of $1,100 to the Hechts in installments before leaving the firm.

The "10-year scheme," lawyers say, is a two-step process, beginning with an asylum application. To qualify for asylum, applicants must show they were persecuted or fear persecution based on race, religion, nationality, membership in a particular social group, or political opinion in their home country. Applications must be filed within a year of arrival, with narrow exceptions.

But the plaintiffs said that neither Thomas Hecht nor Leonard Hecht, who speaks Spanish, asked them specific questions about persecution before filing asylum applications without their knowledge.

Martin Torres Reyes thought that he had found a way to get a green card, but now he is part of a lawsuit that charges a law firm of defrauding him and other immigrants.

Generally, once an applicant is found not to be eligible for asylum, the case is sent to the immigration courts and the deportation process begins. A lawyer can try to get the deportation canceled based on a client's 10-year residency and U.S. citizen children. In some cases, the applicant could be then eligible for a green card, but the bar is very high: "exceptional and extremely unusual hardship" to a U.S. citizen spouse, parent or child if he or she is deported. And even then, only 4,000 of these cases can be approved in a year.

According to federal statistics requested and compiled by the Benjamin N. Cardozo School of Law's immigration clinic, which is a co-counsel in the suit, the Hecht firm had filed 1,039 asylum applications from November 2006 through January 2017. Cardozo said it could only confirm two asylum applications that were approved during that time. The data also shows that the Hechts had subsequently filed 188 applications for "cancellation of removal," and that only six were listed as granted.

The 26 individuals who are plaintiffs in the suit, from Staten Island, the Bronx, Queens and Brooklyn, are now at risk of deportation, as the Trump administration has said that any immigrant living in the United States illegally is a target.

Make the Road New York, an immigrant activist group, is representing Mr. Torres, and is also a plaintiff, suing under the federal racketeering and organized crime act known as RICO. So far, the clients have paid $58,506 to the Hecht firm or to new lawyers to reverse deportation proceedings; the plaintiffs are seeking damages up to three times that amount. The suit also named a Staten Island tax preparer, Luis Guerrero, who steered clients to the law firm, according to the complaint.

At the offices of Thomas T. Hecht, 14 floors above Times Square, his son, Leonard Hecht, 55, was shocked and distraught when confronted with the accusations in the lawsuit late Wednesday. "It's not true," he said firmly. "We didn't do anything fraudulent."

Mr. Hecht insisted that he told his clients that he was applying for asylum on their behalf and that they knew the risks. He said that he only met Mr. Guerrero once, in his office, and that he did not partner with him. He declined to comment further.

There were more than a dozen potential clients waiting to see him on Wednesday. His father, who he said was an 88-year-old Holocaust survivor, was not in the office.

Amy Taylor, the co-legal director of Make the Road New York, said the 10-year myth is pervasive, despite education efforts from her organization and others. "The No. 1 question we get from clients is, 'do I qualify for the 10-year visa?' " Ms. Taylor said. We say, 'there's no such thing, why don't we sit down and explain.' "

The promise seems real to some immigrants at first because of a tangible outcome: six months into a pending asylum application, immigrants are eligible to receive a work permit. Because asylum backlogs can last longer than two years, immigrants would not discover the fraud for a while. And under the Obama administration, they were often allowed to stay in the country even though they were subject to deportation.

For some, applying for asylum and then gambling on a deportation being overturned could be a viable legal strategy, according to Camille Mackler, the legal policy director of the New York Immigration Coalition, an activist group, But she cautioned that was only if a client had a good-faith claim for asylum, a strong fallback case for canceling the removal, and, above all, that the lawyer advised the client of the deportation risk.

E.G.R., 32, a Mexican-born mother of two U.S. citizen children, and one of the plaintiffs, said she did not realize the Hechts had applied for asylum for her until she was told to go to an interview with the government. She asked to be identified only by her initials because she is currently in deportation proceedings.

She said the asylum officer with United States Citizenship and Immigration services asked her, "Why are you asking for political asylum when you've been here so many years?" She was not found eligible for asylum and has a hearing before an immigration court judge on May 18.

E.G.R. said she had been skeptical when her accountant, Mr. Guerrero, first referred her to the Hechts. "I did ask him if this person would steal my money because we worked so hard,' " E.G.R. said. "He said, 'why would you think that? I'm Hispanic as well.' "

Mr. Guerrero did not return a call left at his office.

Lawyers representing the plaintiffs say they are investigating other ways to protect clients thrust into the deportation pipeline, including whether they would be eligible for a visa as victims of fraud.

In a statement, U.S.C.I.S. said it could not address this specific case, but that it has participated in prosecuting recent asylum fraud cases around the country.

What is different about this lawsuit, said Stephen H. Legomsky, a professor of immigration law at Washington University School of Law in St. Louis, is that it "shines a light on the victim," he said, whereas the focus had mostly been on immigrants committing fraud to obtain a benefit. Another of the plaintiffs, who asked to be identified only by her initials, A.M.M., 46, paid the Hecht firm $4,856 and is now in deportation proceedings.

To others who may be tempted by the easy promise of a green card, she has a message: "If something sounds too good to be true, keep an eye out on that."

Trump Moves to End DACA and Calls on Congress to Act

BY MICHAEL D. SHEAR AND JULIE HIRSCHFELD DAVIS | SEPT. 5, 2017

WASHINGTON — President Trump on Tuesday ordered an end to the Obama-era program that shields young undocumented immigrants from deportation, calling it an "amnesty-first approach" and urging Congress to pass a replacement before he begins phasing out its protections in six months.

As early as March, officials said, some of the 800,000 young adults brought to the United States illegally as children who qualify for the program, Deferred Action for Childhood Arrivals, will become eligible for deportation. The five-year-old policy allows them to remain without fear of immediate removal from the country and gives them the right to work legally.

Mr. Trump and Attorney General Jeff Sessions, who announced the change at the Justice Department, both used the aggrieved language of anti-immigrant activists, arguing that those in the country illegally are lawbreakers who hurt native-born Americans by usurping their jobs and pushing down wages.

Mr. Trump said in a statement that he was driven by a concern for "the millions of Americans victimized by this unfair system." Mr. Sessions said the program had "denied jobs to hundreds of thousands of Americans by allowing those same illegal aliens to take those jobs."

Protests broke out in front of the White House and the Justice Department and in cities across the country soon after Mr. Sessions's announcement. Democrats and some Republicans, business executives, college presidents and immigration activists condemned the move as a coldhearted and shortsighted effort that was unfair to the young immigrants and could harm the economy.

"This is a sad day for our country," Mark Zuckerberg, the Facebook founder, wrote on his personal page. "It is particularly cruel to offer young people the American dream, encourage them to come out of the shadows and trust our government, and then punish them for it."

Former President Barack Obama, who had warned that any threat to the program would prompt him to speak out, called his successor's decision "wrong," "self-defeating" and "cruel."

"Whatever concerns or complaints Americans may have about immigration in general, we shouldn't threaten the future of this group of young people who are here through no fault of their own, who pose no threat, who are not taking away anything from the rest of us," Mr. Obama wrote on Facebook.

Both he and Mr. Trump said the onus was now on lawmakers to protect the young immigrants as part of a broader overhaul of the immigration system that would also toughen enforcement. But despite broad and longstanding bipartisan support for measures to legalize unauthorized immigrants brought to the United States as children, the odds of a sweeping immigration deal in a deeply divided Congress appeared long. Legislation to protect the "dreamers" has also repeatedly died in Congress.

Just hours after the angry reaction to Mr. Trump's decision, the president appeared to have second thoughts. In a late-evening tweet, Mr. Trump specifically called on Congress to "legalize DACA," something his administration's officials had declined to do earlier in the day.

Mr. Trump also warned lawmakers that if they do not legislate a program similar to the one Mr. Obama created through executive authority, he will "revisit this issue!" — a statement sure to inject more uncertainty into the ultimate fate of the young, undocumented immigrants who have been benefiting from the program since 2012.

Conservatives praised Mr. Trump's move, though some expressed frustration that he had taken so long to rescind the program and that the gradual phaseout could mean that some immigrants retained protection from deportation until October 2019.

The White House portrayed the decision as a matter of legal necessity, given that nine Republican state attorneys general had threatened to sue to halt the program immediately if Mr. Trump did not act.

Months of internal White House debate preceded the move, as did the president's public display of his own conflicted feelings. He once referred to DACA recipients as "incredible kids."

The president's wavering was reflected in a day of conflicting messages from him and his team. Hours after his statement was released, Mr. Trump told reporters that he had "great love" for the beneficiaries of the program he had just ended. "I have a love for these people, and hopefully now Congress will be able to help them and do it properly," he said. But he notably did not endorse bipartisan legislation to codify the program's protections, leaving it unclear whether he would back such a solution.

Mr. Trump's aides were negotiating late into Monday evening with one another about precisely how the plan to wind down the program would be executed.

Until Tuesday morning, some aides believed the president had settled on a plan that would be more generous, giving more of the program's recipients the option to renew their protections. But even taking into account Mr. Trump's contradictory language, the rollout of his decision was smoother than his early moves to crack down on immigration, particularly the botched execution in January of his ban on travelers from seven predominantly Muslim countries.

In addition to the public statement from Mr. Sessions and a White House question-and-answer session, the president was ready on Tuesday with the lengthy written statement, and officials at the Justice and Homeland Security Departments provided detailed briefings and distributed information to reporters in advance.

Mr. Trump sought to portray his move as a compassionate effort to head off the expected legal challenge that White House officials said would have forced an immediate and highly disruptive end to the program. But he also denounced the policy, saying it helped spark a "massive surge" of immigrants from Central America, some of whom went on to become members of violent gangs like MS-13. Some immigration critics contend that programs like DACA, started under Mr. Obama, encouraged Central Americans to enter the United States, hoping to stay permanently. Tens of thousands of migrants surged across America's southern border in the summer of 2014, many of them children fleeing dangerous gangs.

Sarah Huckabee Sanders, the White House press secretary, indicated that Mr. Trump would support legislation to "fix" the DACA program, as long as Congress passed it as part of a broader immigration overhaul to strengthen the border, protect American jobs and enhance enforcement. "The president wants to see responsible immigration reform, and he wants that to be part of it," Ms. Sanders said, referring to a permanent solution for the young immigrants. "Something needs to be done. It's Congress's job to do that. And we want to be part of that process."

Later on Tuesday, Marc Short, Mr. Trump's top legislative official, told reporters on Capitol Hill that the White House would release principles for such a plan in the coming days, input that at least one key member of Congress indicated would be crucial.

"It is important that the White House clearly outline what kind of legislation the president is willing to sign," Senator Marco Rubio, Republican of Florida, said in a statement. "We have no time to waste on ideas that do not have the votes to pass or that the president won't sign."

The announcement was an effort by Mr. Trump to honor the law-and-order message of his campaign, which included a repeated pledge to end Mr. Obama's immigration policy, while seeking to avoid the emotionally charged and politically perilous consequences of targeting a sympathetic group of immigrants.

Mr. Trump's decision came less than two weeks after he pardoned Joe Arpaio, the former Arizona sheriff who drew intense criticism for his aggressive pursuit of unauthorized immigrants, which earned him a criminal contempt conviction.

The blame-averse president told a confidante over the past few days that he realized that he had gotten himself into a politically untenable position. As late as one hour before the decision was to be announced, administration officials privately expressed concern that Mr. Trump might not fully grasp the details of the steps he was about to take, and when he discovered their full impact, would change his mind, according to a person familiar with their thinking who was not authorized to comment on it and spoke on condition of anonymity.

But ultimately, the president followed through on his campaign pledge at the urging of Mr. Sessions and other hard-line members inside his White House, including Stephen Miller, his top domestic policy adviser. The announcement started the clock on revoking legal status from those protected under the program.

Officials said DACA recipients whose legal status expires on or before March 5 would be able to renew their two-year period of legal status as long as they apply by Oct. 5. But the announcement means that if Congress fails to act, immigrants who were brought to the United States illegally as children could face deportation as early as March 6 to countries where many left at such young ages that they have no memory of them.

Immigration officials said they did not intend to actively target the young immigrants as priorities for deportation, though without the program's protection, they would be considered subject to removal from the United States and would no longer be able to work legally.

Officials said some of the young immigrants could be prevented from returning to the United States if they traveled abroad. Immigration advocates took little comfort from the administration's assurances, describing the president's decision as deeply disturbing and vowing to shift their demands for protections to Capitol Hill.

Marielena Hincapié, the executive director of the National Immigration Law Center, called Mr. Trump's decision "nothing short of hypocrisy, cruelty and cowardice." Maria Praeli, a recipient of protection under the program, criticized Mr. Sessions and Mr. Trump for talking "about us as if we don't matter and as if this isn't our home." The Mexican foreign ministry issued a statement saying the "Mexican government deeply regrets" Mr. Trump's decision.

As recently as July, Mr. Trump expressed skepticism about the prospect of a broad legislative deal. "What I'd like to do is a comprehensive immigration plan," he told reporters. "But our country and political forces are not ready yet."

As for DACA, he said: "There are two sides of a story. It's always tough."

Dreamers' Fate Is Now Tied to Border Wall and Other G.O.P. Immigration Demands

BY ALICIA PARLAPIANO | FEB. 15, 2018

LAWMAKERS HAVE UNTIL March 5 to extend legal protections for Dreamers, the undocumented immigrants who were brought to the United States as children. But the battle over their fate has expanded to include other potential changes to the nation's immigration system, and lawmakers have not come to a consensus.

On Thursday, the Senate voted to advance three different plans, but each failed. Complicating matters, President Trump said Wednesday that he would not support a proposal that did not include the "four pillars" of his own plan: a path to citizenship for Dreamers, a border wall, and an end to the visa lottery system and family-based migration that he calls chain migration. On Thursday, the Department of Homeland Security released a scathing critique of the latest bipartisan plan, which Mr. Trump vowed to veto.

Here is how different proposals address the Dreamers' protections and five other critical issues:

PROTECTIONS FOR DREAMERS

About 700,000 undocumented immigrants are currently shielded from deportation under the Deferred Action for Childhood Arrivals program, or DACA. An additional 1.1 million Dreamers were eligible for the program, but they did not apply. Mr. Trump announced plans to phase out the program by March 5.

Most of the major proposals in Congress include a path to citizenship for Dreamers. One, a more moderate bipartisan Senate proposal introduced by Richard J. Durbin, Democrat of Illinois, and Lindsey Graham, Republican of South Carolina, along with four other senators in the so-called Gang of Six, would also allow parents of Dreamers to obtain three-year renewable legal status.

(That proposal was rejected during a White House meeting in which Mr. Trump reportedly derided people from African nations.)

A more conservative approach, written by the House Judiciary Committee chairman, Robert W. Goodlatte of Virginia, and supported by other Republicans in the House, does not provide a path to citizenship for Dreamers. Instead, it offers three-year renewable legal status for a smaller subset of immigrants who were DACA recipients.

The proposals also differ on who would qualify, potentially expanding protections for more than the 1.8 million immigrants who were eligible for DACA. A narrow bipartisan Senate plan, introduced by John McCain, Republican of Arizona, and Chris Coons, Democrat of Delaware, includes more expansive thresholds for qualification, potentially expanding the number of eligible immigrants to 3.2 million. That plan was voted down Thursday.

In 2001, the Dream Act was introduced to provide a pathway to citizenship for these immigrants without additional immigration measures. Democrats still favor that approach, but it does not have enough support in the Republican-controlled Congress.

BORDER WALL

Mr. Trump has called for full funding, an estimated $25 billion over 10 years, to fulfill his campaign promise to build a wall along the southern border with Mexico, which Democrats have generally opposed. The White House plan has been introduced as legislation by Senator Charles E. Grassley, Republican of Iowa. It would appropriate $25 billion for a border security trust fund, of which $18 billion would go toward a wall and other physical barriers. It was also voted down Thursday.

The House Republican plan "authorizes" about $25 billion for border security, designating $9.3 billion of that for physical barriers like a wall. An authorization is a step taken before an "appropriation," which is actual funding.

The Common Sense Coalition, a bipartisan group of senators led by Susan Collins, Republican of Maine, and Joe Manchin III, Democrat of West Virginia, released a proposal late Wednesday that would appropriate $25 billion for border security overall. On Thursday, the White House released a statement saying that if that plan came to the president's desk, "his advisors would recommend that he veto it." Later, the Senate voted against a motion to advance the plan.

A compromise plan developed by Senator Jeff Flake, Republican of Arizona, addresses the White House's four priorities, including $25 billion for a border security trust fund. The Gang of Six plan would appropriate a total of just $1.6 billion for a border wall. A similar plan has been introduced in the House by the bipartisan Problem Solvers Caucus.

OTHER BORDER SECURITY

Republicans want to beef up security along the border as a condition for other reforms. The House Republican plan takes the most aggressive approach, including a new biometric entry-exit system "at all air, land, and sea ports of entry," with a $15.7 billion authorization for border security on top of money for a wall.

The narrow McCain-Coons plan authorizes (but would not appropriate) a small amount of money ($550 million over 10 years) for border security. That plan is nearly identical to a House bill that has more than 50 bipartisan co-sponsors, but it is not likely to have enough Republican support to pass.

Even the most expensive plans fall short of the border security funding included in the 2013 immigration bill that was passed in the Senate but was never taken up in the House. That compromise bill devoted roughly $40 billion to border security. In exchange, the bill also included a path to citizenship for all 11 million undocumented immigrants in the country, with an expedited path for Dreamers.

INTERIOR ENFORCEMENT

Mr. Trump, along with hard-line Republicans, wants to crack down on unauthorized immigrants with more arrests and faster deportations. The White House plan introduces harsher criminal penalties for deported criminals who re-enter the country and expands the criminal activities that would result in removal for unauthorized immigrants.

The House Republican plan includes many of the same provisions but goes further. It would implement mandatory E-Verify systems for employers, authorize the Justice Department to crack down on so-called sanctuary cities and make visa overstays a federal misdemeanor.

A separate vote to advance an amendment that would withhold federal grants from sanctuary cities failed in the Senate on Thursday. Four Democrats joined the Republicans in supporting it, but they did not reach the 60 votes needed to proceed. None of the other major plans include increased interior enforcement measures.

FAMILY-BASED MIGRATION

Another one of the administration's four priorities is ending "chain migration" — migration that allows legal immigrants to sponsor extended family members. The hard-line plans by the White House and by House Republicans would limit family-based migration to spouses and children and would not reallocate those visas (or would only reallocate a limited number), resulting in less legal immigration over all.

Other plans, from the bipartisan Gang of Six and Senator Flake, also limit family-based migration to spouses and children but redistribute the remaining visas to highly educated and skilled workers or qualifying family. The Common Sense Coalition plan prohibits green card holders from sponsoring adult children. The McCain-Coons plan does not make changes to the visa system.

DIVERSITY VISA LOTTERY

Like the family-based migration changes, ending the diversity visa program is a priority of the Trump administration. The White House plan and the House Republican plan would eliminate the program without redistributing its visas. The Migration Policy Institute, a research organization, estimates that both plans would result in a drop of 30 percent in legal immigration because of their family-based visa and diversity lottery provisions.

Under Senator Flake's plan, diversity lottery visas would be partially reallocated, but the number available would eventually drop off. The Gang of Six plan would also end the program, but would redistribute all of the visas, with some going to vulnerable populations that are in the country under Temporary Protected Status. The McCain-Coons and Common Sense Coalition proposals would keep the program in place.

For Immigrant Students, a New Worry: A Call to ICE

BY ERICA L. GREEN | MAY 30, 2018

HOUSTON — As Dennis Rivera-Sarmiento sat in a detention center 80 miles away from his Texas home this past winter, clad in a blue inmate uniform, he could see his high school diploma slipping further from his reach. Graduation was in June, but a schoolyard scuffle with a girl who he said had called him a racial epithet had gotten him arrested by his high school's police officer.

Then a state law that required the Harris County Sheriff's Office to cooperate with federal immigration officers flagged him for deportation, back to his native Honduras, from which he and his family had fled five years ago.

The case of the "quiet kid who was good at soccer" hauled from high school to a deportation center turned Mr. Rivera-Sarmiento into a cause célèbre in Houston, a textbook case of what immigration advocacy groups fear could happen as schools tighten discipline in the wake of school shootings, the police ratchet up sweeps for gang members and local law enforcement draws closer to the federal immigration authorities.

The school, the community and plenty of lawyers rallied to Mr. Rivera-Sarmiento's side, and on Saturday, he will don a green graduation gown and cross the stage as part of the class of 2018 at Stephen F. Austin High School. But beyond that stage, his future is decidedly uncertain as he awaits an asylum hearing that will determine his future in the United States.

"I actually don't think this is real," Mr. Rivera-Sarmiento, 19, said. "I never thought I'd be graduating. I thought I would be in Honduras right now."

No one is sure how many students like Mr. Rivera-Sarmiento have been channeled from the principal's office to the custody of Immigration and Customs Enforcement. A spokesman for ICE said that the agency cannot track the number of students detained based on school arrests because it does not record how undocumented immigrants are originally arrested.

"Students do not get on ICE's radar; aliens who are criminally arrested by local law enforcement get on ICE's radar," said Carl Rusnok, an agency spokesman.

But immigrant groups think that given the anti-immigrant atmosphere fueled by the Trump administration, the fear is justified. Schools are still widely considered sanctuaries for immigrant students, and educators have been their fiercest advocates. But, said Angie Junck, supervising attorney for the California-based Immigrant Legal Resource Center, "all it takes is one rogue school employee to call ICE."

The agency still classifies schools as "sensitive locations" where enforcement actions are generally prohibited. But immigrant rights groups point out that the designation has not stopped ICE agents from

LOREN ELLIOTT FOR THE NEW YORK TIMES

Mr. Rivera-Sarmiento saw his mug shot while watching the news. He was arrested after a scuffle with a classmate who he says called him a racial epithet.

picking up parents as they drop their children off at school, nor has it prevented school disciplinarians from helping to build ICE cases.

And Education Secretary Betsy DeVos seemed to open the door to more such referrals last week when she initially told members of Congress that ICE enforcement decisions should be left to local officials, not established federal policy that prohibits it. Later she clarified that she expected schools to comply with a 1982 Supreme Court decision that held that schools cannot deny undocumented students an education.

"Schools are not, and should never become, immigration enforcement zones," Ms. DeVos said in a statement on Wednesday. "Every child should feel safe going to school. It is unfortunate that those who seek to polarize and divide have intentionally tried to misrepresent my position on this issue to cause unnecessary fear for students and families."

But as she offered that reassurance, Ms. DeVos moved toward rescinding an Obama-era policy document on student discipline that could make undocumented students vulnerable. That 2014 policy encouraged schools to revise discipline policies that disproportionately kicked students of color out of school.

Data shows that students of color are disproportionately arrested at school, and advocates and educators contend that schools will increasingly rely on law enforcement to manage disciplinary issues if the guidance is rescinded.

In Houston, Mr. Rivera-Sarmiento's run-in with the law still divides the community. Some remain convinced that Mr. Rivera-Sarmiento's status does not exempt him from criminal and immigration laws. Others believe the district unfairly subjected him to them.

Mr. Rivera-Sarmiento said he was arrested at his school after he defended himself against an attack from a schoolmate. She had teased him incessantly, he and his lawyer said, on this day calling him a "wetback" before throwing a bottle of Gatorade at him.

He pushed her down on the ground before running across the street to flee the area. When he returned to the school's campus a few minutes later, he approached the school police officer to report what had happened. He was hoping for help, he said, but was escorted to the principal's office in handcuffs. He was charged with misdemeanor assault.

The officer took him to the county jail, run by the Harris County Sheriff's Office, which is required by state law to cooperate with immigration enforcement. There, he was flagged during booking proceedings as being in the country illegally. Mr. Rivera-Sarmiento, who came to the United States in 2013, had a pending deportation order.

As Mr. Rivera-Sarmiento bounced around three detention centers, students, teachers and advocates held demonstrations, circulated petitions and had fund-raisers to protest his detainment. Mr. Rivera-Sarmiento's plight even caught the attention of Hollywood, where the actress Alyssa Milano signed and publicized a petition with the hashtag #FreeDennis.

Students in the Stephen F. Austin High School community, where 93 percent of students are Hispanic, argued that Mr. Rivera-Sarmiento was also a victim, and that school officials had failed to take into consideration the consequences of an unjustified arrest. "It really raised awareness among our students that this could be any of them," said Cortez Downey, a college counselor at the school. "Already, we have a lot of students in this political climate who wonder if going to school is going to be a waste."

The Houston Independent School District has defended its handling of the episode. In a statement, the district emphasized that Mr. Rivera-Sarmiento had been accused of an "assaultive offense." It added that an incident report said that he had punched his victim in the head, a detail that has been disputed, and that she was taken to a hospital for unspecified injuries. District officials said that they did not report Mr. Rivera-Sarmiento to ICE and have "not used district resources to assist in deportation actions." "Our superintendent and administration remain steadfast in the district's commitment to educating every student regardless of their immigration status," the statement said. "Students are and will continue to be safe in our classrooms."

But Mr. Rivera-Sarmiento's lawyer maintains that the district fell short. "Immigrants have the right to go to school, and schools have the responsibility to take that into account in their policies," said his lawyer, Brandon Roché. "The egregious part is that, especially in a place like Houston, they don't seem to have contemplated this happening."

Mr. Rivera-Sarmiento was released from ICE detention on April 4, on a $2,500 bond.Austin High School's staff, including its principal, vouched in letters that Mr. Rivera-Sarmiento was a good student with no disciplinary issues and needed to be in school.

Mr. Downey said he was stunned when he learned of the arrest. He had met Mr. Rivera-Sarmiento, whom he described as timid, after he was reviewing a list of potentially college-bound students last year and realized that one with a 3.4 grade-point average had not applied to college. Mr. Rivera-Sarmiento went on to secure three acceptances.

Mr. Downey said that Mr. Rivera-Sarmiento's case had taught the school community a lesson. "There's a lot that gets lost in the 'I'm just doing my job' shuffle," Mr. Downey said. "And we realize what that means now."

Upon his return to school, Mr. Rivera-Sarmiento was welcomed with hugs. Sitting at his home after his first day back, he maintained that he loved school, that it was the only place where he felt he could be himself. "I didn't mean for any of this to happen; I just tried to protect myself," he said. "But they say they have to protect the country, and this is not my country. I respect that."

Mr. Rivera-Sarmiento is awaiting a hearing date for his immigration case, where his lawyer will seek asylum. Until then, he plans to enroll in college — the first in his family to do so.

Judge Upholds Order for Trump Administration to Restore DACA

BY MIRIAM JORDAN | AUG. 3, 2018

A FEDERAL JUDGE on Friday upheld his previous order to revive an Obama-era program that shields some 700,000 young immigrants from deportation, saying that the Trump administration had failed to justify eliminating it.

Judge John D. Bates of the Federal District Court for the District of Columbia gave the government 20 days to appeal his decision. But his ruling could conflict with another decision on the program that a federal judge in Texas is expected to issue as early as next week.

The Trump administration announced late last year that it would phase out the program known as Deferred Action for Childhood Arrivals, or DACA, which protects undocumented young adults from deportation and grants them two-year renewable work permits. The administration argued that President Barack Obama had overstepped his authority and circumvented Congress when he created the program in 2012.

The decision to end the program has faced numerous legal challenges. Currently, the government must continue accepting applications to renew DACA status, if not new applications from those who meet the criteria to qualify. DACA recipients — often called "Dreamers" — typically were brought to the United States illegally as children through no choice of their own.

Judge Bates ruled in late April that the administration must restore the DACA program and accept new applications. He had stayed his decision for 90 days to give the Department of Homeland Security, which runs the program, the opportunity to lay out its reasons for ending it.

Kirstjen Nielsen, the homeland security secretary, responded last month, arguing that DACA would likely be found unconstitutional in the Texas case and therefore must end. She relied heavily on the memorandum that her predecessor, Elaine C. Duke, had issued to rescind the program and said that the department had the discretion to end the program, just as the department under Mr. Obama had exercised discretion to create it.

Judge Bates, who was appointed by President George W. Bush, did not agree. He called the shutdown of the program "arbitrary and capricious" and said that Secretary Nielsen's response "fails to elaborate meaningfully on the agency's primary rationale for its decision."

Two federal judges, in Brooklyn and in San Francisco, issued injunctions this year ordering the government to keep the program. But neither of those rulings required that the government accept new applications, as the ruling by Judge Bates does. The earlier decisions are pending before appeals courts.

Meanwhile, the State of Texas and several other plaintiffs have sued the government to rescind the program, contending that it is illegal.

The District of Columbia lawsuit was brought by the N.A.A.C.P., Microsoft and Princeton University. The DACA program has broad bipartisan support in the business and academic worlds.

Christopher L. Eisgruber, the president of Princeton, hailed the court's decision. "Princeton University's continued success as a world-class institution of learning and research depends on our ability to attract talent from all backgrounds, including Dreamers," he said. Brad Smith, the president of Microsoft, said that finding a solution for DACA "has become an economic imperative and a humanitarian necessity."

Since the 2016 presidential campaign, the young people who benefited from DACA have seen their hopes alternately elevated and dashed, sometimes in the space of a week. Neither a flurry of court decisions nor horse-trading in Congress has settled the issue.

In a statement on Friday, United We Dream, an organization that represents Dreamers, offered a sobering assessment: "The situation for DACA beneficiaries remains dangerous and unstable, as we do not know how the administration will respond, and there are other court cases in progress."

CHAPTER 4

Families at the Border

Under the Trump administration, the United States has debated immigration policy, travel bans, a border wall and separating migrant families at the Mexico–United States border. In May 2018, the administration implemented a "zero-tolerance" immigration policy that was meant to deter illegal immigration from Central America. Concerns about separated families, detention centers, deportation and misinformation flooded headlines as activity at the border was investigated.

Hundreds of Immigrant Children Have Been Taken From Parents at U.S. Border

BY CAITLIN DICKERSON | APRIL 20, 2018

ON FEB. 20, a young woman named Mirian arrived at the Texas border carrying her 18-month-old son. They had fled their home in Honduras through a cloud of tear gas, she told border agents, and needed protection from the political violence there. She had hoped she and her son would find refuge together. Instead, the agents ordered her to place her son in the back seat of a government vehicle, she said later in a sworn declaration to a federal court. They both cried as the boy was driven away.

For months, members of Congress have been demanding answers about how many families are being separated as they are processed at stations along the southwest border, in part because the Trump administration has in the past said it was considering taking children from their parents as a way to deter migrants from coming here. Officials have repeatedly declined to provide data on how many families have been separated, but suggested that the number was relatively low.

But new data reviewed by The New York Times shows that more than 700 children have been taken from adults claiming to be their parents since October, including more than 100 children under the age of 4.

The data was prepared by the Office of Refugee Resettlement, a division of the Department of Health and Human Services that takes custody of children who have been removed from migrant parents. Senior officials at the Department of Homeland Security, which processes migrants at the border, initially denied that the numbers were so high. But after they were confirmed to The Times by three federal officials who work closely with these cases, a spokesman for the health and human services department on Friday acknowledged in a statement that there were "approximately 700."

Homeland security officials said the agency does not separate families at the border for deterrence purposes. "As required by law, D.H.S. must protect the best interests of minor children crossing our borders, and occasionally this results in separating children from an adult they are traveling with if we cannot ascertain the parental relationship, or if we think the child is otherwise in danger," a spokesman for the agency said in a statement.

But Trump administration officials have suggested publicly in the past that they were, indeed, considering a deterrence policy. Last year, John F. Kelly, President Trump's chief of staff, floated the idea while he was serving as homeland security secretary. If approved, the plan would have closed detention facilities that are designed to house families and replaced them with separate shelters for adults and children. The White House supported the move and convened a group of officials from several federal agencies to consider its merits. But the Department of Homeland Security has said the policy was never adopted.

Children removed from their families are taken to shelters run by nongovernmental organizations. There, workers seek to identify a relative or guardian in the United States who can take over the child's care. But if no such adult is available, the children can languish in custody indefinitely. Operators of these facilities say they are often unable to locate the parents of separated children because the children arrive without proper records.

Once a child has entered the shelter system, there is no firm process to determine whether they have been separated from someone who was legitimately their parent, or for reuniting parents and children who had been mistakenly separated, said a Border Patrol official, who was not authorized to discuss the agency's policies publicly.

"The idea of punishing parents who are trying to save their children's lives, and punishing children for being brought to safety by their parents by separating them, is fundamentally cruel and un-American," said Michelle Brané, director of the Migrant Rights and Justice program at the Women's Refugee Commission, an advocacy group that conducts interviews and monitoring at immigration detention centers, including those that house children. "It really to me is just a horrific 'Sophie's Choice' for a mom."

Mirian has pinballed across Texas, held at various times in three other detention centers. She is part of a lawsuit filed by the American Civil Liberties Union on behalf of many immigrant parents seeking to prohibit family separations at the border.

Her son's name, along with Mirian's surname, are being withheld for their safety. But in a declaration she filed in that case, she said she was never told why her son was being taken away from her. Since February, the only word she has received about him has come from a case manager at the facility in San Antonio where he is being held. Her son asked about her and "cried all the time" in the days after he arrived at the facility, the case worker said, adding that the boy had developed an ear infection and a cough.

"I had no idea that I would be separated from my child for seeking help," Mirian said in her sworn statement. "I am so anxious to be reunited with him."

Protecting children at the border is complicated because there have, indeed, been instances of fraud. Tens of thousands of migrants arrive there every year, and those with children in tow are often released into the United States more quickly than adults who come alone, because of restrictions on the amount of time that minors can be held in custody. Some migrants have admitted they brought their children not only to remove them from danger in such places as Central America and Africa, but because they believed it would cause the authorities to release them from custody sooner. Others have admitted to posing falsely with children who are not their own, and Border Patrol officials say that such instances of fraud are increasing.

As the debate carries on, pressure from the White House to enact a separation policy has continued. In conversations this month with Kirstjen Nielsen, the homeland security secretary, Mr. Trump has repeatedly expressed frustration that the agency has not been aggressive enough in policing the border, according to a person at the White House who is familiar with the discussions.

Officials presented Mr. Trump with a list of proposals, including the plan to routinely separate immigrant adults from their children. The president urged Ms. Nielsen to move forward with the policies, the person said.

But even groups that support stricter immigration policies have stopped short of endorsing a family separation policy. Jessica M. Vaughan, the director of policy studies for the Center for Immigration Studies, one such group, said that family separation should only be used as a "last resort." However, she said that some migrants were using children as "human shields" in order to get out of immigration custody faster.

"It makes no sense at all for the government to just accept these attempts at fraud," Ms. Vaughan said. "If it appears that the child is being used in this way, it is in the best interest of the child to be kept separately from the parent, for the parent to be prosecuted, because it's a crime and it's one that has to be deterred and prosecuted."

Trump Administration Threatens Jail and Separating Children From Parents for Those Who Illegally Cross Southwest Border

BY MIRIAM JORDAN AND RON NIXON | MAY 7, 2018

LOS ANGELES — The Trump administration announced Monday that it is dramatically stepping up prosecutions of those who illegally cross the Southwest border, ramping up a "zero tolerance" policy intended to deter new migrants with the threat of jail sentences and separating immigrant children from their parents.

"If you cross the Southwest border unlawfully, then we will prosecute you. It's that simple," Attorney General Jeff Sessions said in announcing a policy that will impose potential criminal penalties on border crossers who previously faced mainly civil deportation proceedings — and in the process, force the separation of families crossing the border for months or longer.

The new policy could flood the immigration courts, already suffering severe backlogs, and create new detention space shortages for federal agencies that even now have been forced to release many undocumented immigrants until their cases can be heard. Mr. Sessions said he has dispatched 35 additional prosecutors and 18 immigration judges to the Southwest border region to help handle expanding caseloads.

The stepped-up enforcement strategy marks the Trump administration's toughest move yet to stem the flow of migrants into the United States, though officials said the category of migrants accounting for much of the recent surge, those seeking asylum from violence in Central America, will still be able to apply for legal refuge.

"Today we're here to send a message to the world that we are not going to let the country be overwhelmed. People are not going to caravan or otherwise stampede our border," Mr. Sessions said in the second of a pair of announcements in Arizona and California.

The new policy strikes squarely at parents who have traveled with their children, some apparently with the expectation that they would face shorter periods of detention while their cases were heard.

"If you are smuggling a child then we will prosecute you, and that child will be separated from you as required by law," Mr. Sessions said at a law enforcement conference in Scottsdale, Ariz. "If you don't like that, then don't smuggle children over our border."

The new initiative will result in referring all illegal Southwest border crossings to the Justice Department for prosecution, Mr. Sessions said, and federal prosecutors will file charges in as many cases as possible "until we get to 100 percent."

Under current law, anyone crossing illegally into the country can be prosecuted, and the penalties are even stiffer if they attempt to enter the country after they have been deported. In most cases, though, first-time offenders are simply put into civil deportation proceedings. While it is unlikely that Mr. Sessions' goal of 100 percent prosecutions will be achieved, officials at the Department of Homeland Security say they want to significantly increase the number of people referred for criminal prosecution.

"What is notable about this is that they are taking into criminal proceedings first-time crossers, which has generally not been the case in the past," said Doris Meissner, senior fellow at the Migration Policy Institute, who served as immigration commissioner during the Clinton administration.

A similar zero-tolerance policy was attempted in 2005 in parts of Texas and Arizona under the George W. Bush administration, which ordered criminal prosecutions of immigrants in those areas who entered the country illegally. The policy lasted into the Obama administration before it was scaled back.

Another pilot prosecution project was implemented in the El Paso area at the beginning of the 2017 fiscal year. The number of illegal crossings of families dropped by 64 percent, according to Immigration and Customs Enforcement officials, who said entries began rising again after the initiative ended.

During the first six months of the fiscal year 2018, there were 35,787 criminal prosecutions for immigration violations, according to data from the Transactional Records Access Clearinghouse, a research group at Syracuse University. If prosecutions continue at that pace for the rest of the year, it would be a 19.5 percent increase in prosecutions compared to fiscal 2017, the American Immigration Council said.

The proposal has been in discussion for some time by top officials at the Department of Homeland Security. Under the directive, undocumented immigrants who are stopped by the Border Patrol or customs officers will be sent directly to a federal court by the United States Marshals Service. Children will be placed in the custody of Health and Human Services' Office of Refugee Resettlement, administration officials said.

The adult immigrants would be sent to detention centers to await trial. If convicted, they would be imprisoned for the duration of their sentences, after which time they could be returned to their countries of origin. First-time illegal entry is a misdemeanor that carries up to a six-month prison sentence. Repeat entry constitutes a felony and carries a penalty of up to two years imprisonment.

After a lull, the number of women and children making the perilous journey over land from Central America to the United States has spiked. Many of them are fleeing gangs, which often try to recruit their children. Honduras, the source of many of the migrants, has among the world's highest murder rate.

The number of border apprehensions totaled 50,924 in April 2018 compared with 15,766 the same month last year. But the 2018 figure was roughly the same as that of April 2016, suggesting that 2017 was an outlier. Last month, nearly 10,000 people traveling in families were apprehended at the border, and almost 50,000 have been arrested since October, the start of the fiscal year.

"Right now we are dealing with a massive influx of illegal aliens across our Southwest border. In April we saw triple the number from last April," said Mr. Sessions. "But we're not going to stand for this."

But the overall flow of undocumented immigrants remains low compared to previous years. In fiscal year 2017, the Border Patrol apprehended 303,916 people compared to 408,870 in fiscal 2016, 331,333 in 2015 and 479,371 in fiscal 2014.

"Yes, we have this spike in Central Americans. But the overall undocumented flow is at historic lows," said Seth Stodder, a former assistant secretary of Homeland Security in the Obama administration who also served as policy director for Customs and Border Protection during the Bush administration.

"We are not facing a 'massive influx' of undocumented migrants coming across the US-Mexico border. In fact, the opposite is true — undocumented migrant crossings are at historic lows, with border apprehensions around 20 percent of what they were around the time of the 9/11 attacks," Mr. Stodder said.

Under United States and international law, asylum seekers are afforded the opportunity to seek protection, and the overloaded immigration courts are not up to the challenge, he added. "Brutally separating young children from their parents is not a response worthy of a great and humane nation," Mr. Stodder said.

The Trump administration already had hinted that a policy of separating migrant children from their parents was under consideration as a means of deterrence.

Officials have insisted no such policy is in place, though about 700 children, including 100 children four years old and younger, have been separated from their parents since October, according to the Department of Health and Human Services refugee office. The new policy will surely increase this number.

Leaders of a caravan of migrants that recently arrived at the California-Mexico border and that President Trump has vowed to keep from entering the country were critical of the new policy.

"The U.S. Government is waging a war on refugee families that has reached a new level of heartlessness and hate," said Alex Mensing, a spokesman for the organizing group, from Pueblo Sin Fronteras. "Sessions' attack on the rights of refugees violates both U.S. law and international agreements, not to mention the spirit of welcoming those fleeing violence and in need of refuge," he added. "Refugee parents aren't smuggling their children, they're saving their lives."

Jenna Gilbert, a managing attorney in Los Angeles for Human Rights First, a nonprofit that represents asylum seekers and other immigrants, accused the administration of attempting to frighten people out of seeking a safe haven in the United States. "Separating mothers and children at the border is just another example of the administration's cruelty and attempts to scare or deter people from seeking asylum, " Ms. Gilbert said.

However, immigrants seeking asylum still could be protected, the officials said. The new policy, meant to deter illegal immigration, would not apply to people who present themselves at ports of entry seeking asylum. In cases where migrants who have illegally entered the United States express fear of returning to their home country because of political prosecution or other dangers, Customs and Border Protection officers can refer them to asylum interviews.

Other critics warned that the new policy is logistically unworkable. "If they try to prosecute all these folks for illegal immigration it will overwhelm the federal courts," said Royce Murray, policy director at the American Immigration Council, a nonprofit group in Washington.

Did the Trump Administration Separate Immigrant Children From Parents and Lose Them?

BY AMY HARMON | MAY 28, 2018

PRESIDENT TRUMP over the weekend falsely blamed Democrats for a "horrible law" separating immigrant children from their parents. In fact, his own administration had just announced this policy earlier this month.

His comments followed days of growing alarm that federal authorities have lost track of more than 1,000 immigrant children, mostly from Central America, giving rise to hashtags like #WhereAreTheChildren and claims that children are being ripped from their parents' arms at the border and then being lost.

But the president is not the only one spreading wrong information. Across social media, there have been confusing reports of what happened to these immigrant children. Here are some answers.

Did the Trump administration separate nearly 1,500 immigrant children from their parents at the border, and then lose track of them?

No. The government did realize last year that it lost track of 1,475 migrant children it had placed with sponsors in the United States, according to testimony before a Senate subcommittee last month. But those children had arrived alone at the Southwest border — without their parents. Most of them are from Honduras, El Salvador and Guatemala, and were fleeing drug cartels, gang violence and domestic abuse, according to government data.

Officials at the Department of Health and Human Services, which oversees refugee resettlement, began making calls last year to determine what had happened to 7,635 children the government had helped place between last October and the end of the year.

From these calls, officials learned that 6,075 children remained with their sponsors. Twenty-eight had run away, five had been removed from the United States and 52 had relocated to live with a nonsponsor. The rest were unaccounted for, giving rise to the 1,475 number. It is possible that some of the adult sponsors simply chose not to respond to the agency.

Losing track of children who arrive at the border alone is not a new phenomenon. A 2016 inspector general report showed that the federal government was able to reach only 84 percent of children it had placed, leaving 4,159 unaccounted for.

On Monday evening, Eric Hargan, the deputy secretary for Health and Human Services, expressed frustration at the use of the term "lost" to refer to the 1,475 unaccounted-for children. In a statement, he said that the department's office of refugee resettlement began voluntarily making the calls as a 30-day follow-up to make sure that the children and their sponsors did not require additional services. Those calls, which the office does not view as required, Mr. Hargan said, are now "being used to confuse and spread misinformation." In many cases, the statement said, sponsors cannot be reached because "they themselves are illegal aliens and do not want to be reached by federal authorities."

What is the Trump administration's policy on separating migrant children from their parents at the border?

This is where people are likely getting the idea that the Trump administration has separated children from their parents and then lost them. Attorney General Jeff Sessions announced a new "zero tolerance" policy earlier this month that included imposing criminal penalties meant to deter Central American families from trying to cross the border illegally.

If a mother or father is with a child when apprehended for the crime of illegal entry, the minor must be taken from the parent. Hundreds of immigrant children have already been separated from their parents at the border since October, and the new policy will result in a steep increase. "If you don't want your child separated, then don't bring them across the border illegally," Mr. Sessions said. It's not clear what has happened to the children that have been separated from their parents since October.

What about Trump's tweet suggesting that Americans pressure Democrats 'to end the horrible law that separates children from parents at the border'?

There is no law mandating separation. The closest is the Trump administration's own "zero tolerance" policy. And the Democrats did not initiate that.

How did the Department of Health and Human Services manage to lose track of 1,475 migrant children?

Children who show up at the border by themselves are usually apprehended by federal agents. Once they are processed, they are turned over to the custody of the Department of Health and Human Services' refugee office, which provides care until they can be turned over to a sponsor. Sponsors, usually parents or family members already residing in the United States, are supposed to undergo a detailed background check. Historically, the agency has said it was not legally responsible for children after they had been released from its refugee office. But Congress is now examining the agency's safeguards.

Why might the government want to track migrant children?

After being placed with a sponsor, unaccompanied minors face deportation proceedings. They may seek asylum or other relief to try to remain in the country legally.

Senator Rob Portman, Republican of Ohio and chairman of a Senate Homeland Security subcommittee, has said the government has a responsibility to track them so that they are not abused or trafficked, and so that they attend their court proceedings. In 2016, under the Obama administration, the subcommittee released a report finding that department officials had failed to establish procedures to protect unaccompanied minors from being turned over to smugglers or human traffickers. Eight children, the report found, had been placed with human traffickers who forced them to work on an egg farm.

To prevent similar episodes, the Homeland Security and Health and Human Services Departments agreed to establish new guidelines within a year. It is now more than a year after that deadline.

What will happen to children separated from their parents under the new 'zero tolerance' policy?

Undocumented immigrants who are stopped by the Border Patrol or customs officers will be sent directly to a federal court by the United States Marshals Service. Children will be placed in the custody of Health and Human Services' Office of Refugee Resettlement, administration officials said — the same office that handles minors who show up at the border unaccompanied by an adult. The adult immigrants would be sent to detention centers to await trial.

If convicted, immigrants would be imprisoned for the duration of their sentences, after which time they could be returned to their countries of origin. First-time illegal entry is a misdemeanor that carries up to a six-month prison sentence. Repeat entry constitutes a felony and carries a penalty of up to two years' imprisonment. It is not clear how easily they would be able to reunite with their children.

More Than 450 Migrant Parents May Have Been Deported Without Their Children

BY MIRIAM JORDAN AND CAITLIN DICKERSON | JULY 24, 2018

WASHINGTON — The Trump administration told a federal court on Tuesday that more than 450 migrant parents whose children were separated from them are no longer in the United States, raising questions about whether the parents fully understood that they were being deported without their children.

The parents — nearly one-fifth of the 2,551 migrants whose children were taken from them after crossing the southwest border — were either swiftly deported or somehow left the country without their children, government lawyers said.

The exact number, 463, is still "under review," the lawyers added, and could change. However, the disclosure was the first time the government has acknowledged that hundreds of migrant families face formidable barriers of bureaucracy and distance that were unforeseen in the early stages of the government's "zero-tolerance" policy on border enforcement.

The government's previous estimate of the number of such cases was just 12, though that applied only to parents of the youngest children.

"We are extremely worried that a large percentage of parents may already have been removed without their children," said Lee Gelernt, a lawyer with the American Civil Liberties Union, which is challenging the government's handling of migrant children in a lawsuit. He said further clarification was needed to understand just what has happened.

Facing a court-ordered deadline of Thursday, federal agencies must reunite more than 1,500 migrant parents with their children within about 48 hours. Those parents are just a portion of the total number who were separated: those who have been deemed eligible after a background check and a confirmation of where they are in the United States or abroad.

Elsa Ortiz was deported to Guatemala from the United States in June after being separated from her 8-year-old son.

Returning children even to eligible parents has been messy and has revealed challenges facing the government as it complies with the judicial order. For example, reunifications at the Port Isabel detention center in South Texas screeched to a halt on Sunday after it was locked down for five hours, according to Carlos Garcia, an immigration lawyer who was prevented from entering the building to meet with his clients. The lockdown resulted from an accidental miscounting of detainees there, Mr. Garcia said.

It was only the latest hiccup at Port Isabel, where parents, children and their advocates have had to wait for hours, or even days, for reunification. "It's a mess," a person familiar with the reunification process said on Tuesday, adding that "the wait times have been enormous."

The person said that the children's escorts have had to request hotel rooms, which have been approved by the Health and Human Services Department, the agency that oversees care of the separated children.

Among the migrants inside Port Isabel during Sunday's lockdown was Irma, a 35-year-old woman from Honduras separated for more than two months from her two teenage sons, Fernando and Jonatan.

Irma, who asked that only her first name be used, hadn't thought a reunion would happen. A federal official had told her she would never see the boys again.

"It was horrible, horrible," Irma said through tears on Tuesday, inside the airport in McAllen, Tex. The family was about to board a flight to Baltimore.

The hurdles that remain in the reunification process were discussed at a status hearing on Tuesday, where little more was explained about the number of parents who appear to have left or have been sent out of the country without their children.

The judge who ordered the reunifications, Dana M. Sabraw of Federal District Court in San Diego, called the situation the "unfortunate" result of a policy that was introduced "without forethought to reunification or keeping track of people."

Some immigrant advocates said many of the migrant parents had agreed to be deported quickly, believing that doing so would speed up reunification — and perhaps not understanding that they would be leaving their children behind.

"Our attorney volunteers working with detained separated parents are seeing lots of people who signed forms that they didn't understand," said Taylor Levy, a legal coordinator at Annunciation House in El Paso, which assists migrants. "They thought the only way they would see their child again is by agreeing to deportation."

"It is particularly problematic for indigenous Guatemalans who are not fluent in Spanish and were not given explanations in their native languages," Ms. Levy added.

Border authorities are pressuring people to accept speedy deportation, immigration lawyers and advocates say.

"We are aware of instances in which parents have felt coerced and didn't fully understand the consequences of signing or did not feel they had a choice in the matter," said Marielena Hincapié, executive director of the National Immigration Law Center, which represents migrants.

In an attempt to stanch the flow of undocumented immigrants, the Trump administration in May launched a policy under which every adult caught entering the country illegally was subject to criminal prosecution. As part of the crackdown, some 3,000 children were removed from their parents.

Following an international outcry, President Trump signed an executive order on June 20 halting the separations. Judge Sabraw then issued an order that all the families be reunified within about 30 days — a deadline that expires on Thursday.

The authorities have been transporting parents and children to staging areas in Texas, New Mexico and Arizona. After reunification, a variety of nonprofit organizations help the families reach various destinations around the country to await further hearings in immigration court. Hundreds of volunteers are involved in the effort, which includes offering temporary accommodation, airfare and other assistance.

But the swift pace of reunifications has also prompted concerns that the legal cases, health or safety of the parents and children could suffer. The Legal Aid Society of New York filed habeas petitions on Tuesday preventing nine separated children from being moved out of New York until they and their lawyers can contact their parents to determine what's best for the children. The petitions were transferred to San Diego and combined with the lawsuit there over family separation.

The court filings explained the cases of four siblings who want to be reunited with their mother, but not if it would lead to them all being deported to Honduras, where they fear for their lives. The filings also tells of a 9-year-old girl from El Salvador who does not want to return to a detention center where she was traumatized after being made to eat spoiled food, and of the mother of a 9-year-old boy from Honduras, who fears that if he joins her in detention, he won't get his medication for hyperactivity.

The filings, which claim the rights of the children are being denied, were made because of a lawsuit Legal Aid filed last week in Federal District Court in Manhattan that ordered immigration authorities to give 48 hours' notice to lawyers before moving clients. That case, too, was moved to federal court in San Diego.

Judge Sabraw last week temporarily suspended the deportation of reunited families, but immigration lawyers have reported that many of their clients have been funneled to family detention facilities rather than released, which indicates that they could be deported once the judge's stay is lifted.

A spokesman for the Justice Department said the government does not comment on ongoing litigation.

Immigration officials have said that all the parents who were deported without their children made an informed decision to do so, and had agreed in writing to leave their offspring in the United States. The administration said that bilingual workers and interpreters are on hand to help.

Some Central American migrants are illiterate. And many migrants from the highlands of Guatemala, where several dialects are spoken, do not speak Spanish.

The government said in its filing that it has reunited 879 parents with their children. Another 538 parents have been cleared for reunions and are still awaiting transportation.

In accordance with the court order, the administration first began by reunifying 102 parents whose children are 5 or younger. It is currently reunifying the larger group, which includes minors age 5 to 17.

In cases where parents choose to leave the country without their child, they appoint a sponsor — typically a relative — to care for the child. The sponsors undergo extensive background checks before they can take custody. In the meantime, the minors remain in shelters.

LIZ ROBBINS contributed reporting from New York, MANNY FERNANDEZ from Falfurrias, Tex., and MITCHELL FERMAN from McAllen, Tex.

Migrant Families Have Been Reunited. Now, a Scramble to Prevent Deportations.

BY MIRIAM JORDAN | JULY 30, 2018

LOS ANGELES — The federal government last week completed reunifications of more than 1,800 migrant families separated under the Trump administration's "zero-tolerance" policy, but immigrant advocates were set to be back in court Tuesday to block what they said was another imminent threat: plans to swiftly deport up to 1,000 of the newly reunited families.

In separate filings in San Diego and Washington, lawyers asked the courts to order a stay on deporting any of these families and to make sure parents are allowed to remain in the United States as long as needed to help their children pursue claims for asylum from unsafe conditions in Central America.

Judge Paul Friedman of the Federal District Court of the District of Columbia scheduled a hearing Tuesday on a request for a temporary restraining order to halt what could be hundreds of removals for parents who have already exhausted their immigration appeals — but whose children may well have better cases for remaining in the country.

Nearly 3,000 children were forcibly separated from their parents under the "zero-tolerance" immigration policy carried out earlier this year.

Critics say that many parents have been confused or coerced into signing forms that waive their children's right to asylum in the hope of being reunited with them quickly. The latest court filings argue that parents have a right to remain in the country and help their children pursue their asylum cases.

"We want to make sure these kids are not summarily deported before they have a chance to apply for asylum. Their parents in many

Immigrant rights activists rallied outside the federal courthouse in McAllen, Tex., last week. The government has completed reunifications of more than 1,800 migrant families separated under the "zero-tolerance" policy.

instances are the only ones able to articulate their fear," said T. Clark Weymouth, pro bono partner at the international law firm that filed the case in Washington, Hogan Lovells.

Judge Dana M. Sabraw is considering a similar issue in the Federal District Court in San Diego. He is also considering the fate of an estimated 711 children who could not be reunited with their families because their parents were for various reasons deemed "ineligible," including more than 460 parents who were most likely deported already without their children.

Government lawyers have argued that all parents were allowed to choose whether to waive asylum for their children and leave the country with them or allow the children to remain behind and pursue asylum cases. The Trump administration has accused adult migrants of using their children to secure entry into the United States.

Several lawyers for the latest plaintiffs spent time at detention facilities in recent weeks, Mr. Weymouth said, and concluded that without the legal challenge, there would be no impediment to the government deporting the children with their parents as quickly as possible.

"We had signals that was about to happen," said Zachary Best, one of the lawyers.

The reason that children have different prospects for asylum protection has to do with the way immigration authorities handled their cases when they were separated from their parents at the border. Under the "zero-tolerance" policy, anyone who illegally crossed the border outside of a legal entry station has been referred for possible criminal prosecution. Under the previous family separation policy, later rescinded by President Trump, any child accompanying the adult was taken away and designated as an "unaccompanied alien child," a classification normally used for adolescents who arrive at the border alone.

As a result of that designation, children are eligible for legal remedies independent of their parents. They can make an asylum claim before a judge and remain in the country until their case has moved through an immigration court, a process that can take years. If they do not demonstrate a credible fear of persecution in their home country on an initial interview, adults are often targeted for quick deportation. Adults who illegally cross the border, as opposed to surrendering to Border Patrol agents at a legal port of entry, are often not permitted to apply for asylum, though immigrant advocates have argued that they should legally be entitled to do so.

So complicated has the deportation issue become that it now appears that some parents who were reunited with their children in recent weeks have been separated from them once again — this time because they expressed a desire to allow their child to pursue an asylum claim.

A legal filing over the weekend alleges that several fathers, after being reunited with their adolescent children, were given three choices: to be deported with their children; be deported alone and allow their children to stay; or wait to consult a lawyer. They said that the first option had been pre-selected for them when they were handed the forms.

When they tried to choose the second option — to be removed from the country alone and allow their children to stay behind to pursue a separate asylum case — agents with Immigration and Customs Enforcement became angry at them, the fathers said in their court challenge.

The problem with the waiver form, their lawyers argued, is that it did not make the consequences clear — that by selecting the option to be deported with their child, a parent was waiving the child's right to pursue asylum. In the case of the fathers, all chose to be deported alone. In their declarations, they said they were not allowed to say goodbye to their children. The children, they said, had to wave to them from inside a bus.

CHAPTER 5

Global Impact

Immigration, legal and illegal, is not just a question that affects the United States. Countries all over the world are grappling with their own immigration issues, especially as people flee from wars and harsh governments or climate conditions that make their lives intolerable. How will the world handle this increasing number of immigrants, and how will the newer and more stringent U.S. policies toward immigration affect other countries?

Nations Hinder U.S. Effort to Deport Immigrants Convicted of Crime

BY RON NIXON | JULY 1, 2016

WASHINGTON — Thousands of immigrants with criminal convictions, including for assault and attempted murder, have been released from detention because their native countries refused to take them back, according to statistics recently released by the Department of Homeland Security.

The inability to deport the criminals has prompted outrage among lawmakers and advocates of tighter immigration laws, who say that the Obama administration could be doing much more to pressure uncooperative countries.

But the department faces a number of obstacles. It is legally barred from indefinitely detaining immigrants who cannot be repatriated. And poorer nations are often reluctant to take back violent offenders because they have limited resources to deal with them.

The release of such immigrants into American cities is a particularly charged aspect of the national debate over immigration. Donald J. Trump, the presumptive Republican presidential nominee, has painted a grim picture of immigrant criminals menacing the streets.

More than 100 of the immigrants released by the government have later been charged in homicides. In one of the most recent examples, Jean Jacques, a Haitian immigrant, was sentenced last month to 60 years in prison for the murder of Casey Chadwick, a 25-year-old woman from Norwich, Conn.

Mr. Jacques, who previously served time for attempted murder, had been released in 2012 after the immigration agency tried several times to deport him. Haitian officials blocked the transfer because they said Mr. Jacques could not prove that he was a citizen.

Records recently released by Immigration and Customs Enforcement, the agency responsible for deportations, show that more than 8,000 immigrants with criminal convictions in the United States have been set free here since 2013. The figures, requested by Congress, include both undocumented immigrants and some with legal status.

Lawmakers, calling the issue a threat to public safety, said it was appalling that Haiti and other countries had prevented the deportations. "There is no reason we should have to go on bended knee to ask them," said Senator Richard Blumenthal, Democrat of Connecticut. "We shouldn't have to keep someone in this country who is here illegally but also dangerous."

Mr. Blumenthal said he planned to introduce legislation that would impose sanctions on countries that refuse to take back their nationals.

Senator Charles E. Grassley, Republican of Iowa, urged Jeh Johnson, the secretary of Homeland Security, in a letter this week to do more to press recalcitrant countries. "Lives are being lost," Mr. Grassley wrote. "It can't continue."

Immigration officials say their hands are tied. In 2001, the Supreme Court ruled that the Fifth Amendment's guarantee of due process barred the government from detaining immigrants indefinitely simply for lack of a country willing to take them.

The Clinton and Bush administrations had argued that immigration law authorized, and that the Constitution permitted, indefinite detention of immigrants unable to be repatriated. But the court ruled that after six months of detention, if deportation did not seem very likely in the near future, the government would have to offer special reasons for keeping someone in custody.

"The six-month requirement makes it very difficult to hold on to these people," Mr. Johnson told senators at a Senate Judiciary Committee hearing on Thursday.

But experts say the federal government has a number of options to persuade countries to take back their citizens. The immigration authorities can hold immigrants longer if they can show that they pose a risk to public safety, like a threat of terrorism. And under the law, the State Department can deny visas to nationals of countries that refuse to repatriate their citizens.

But a 2004 study by the Government Accountability Office found that the department had used that option just once, in 2001 against the South American nation of Guyana. The State Department declined to say whether it had denied visas in this manner since 2004.

Katherine M. Pfaff, a spokeswoman for the State Department, said it worked with the Department of Homeland Security to try to resolve issues with countries in individual immigration cases.

Jon Feere, an analyst at the Center for Immigration Studies, which favors stricter immigration rules, said the State Department was putting diplomacy ahead of security.

"Public safety seems to have taken a back seat to concerns about upsetting relations with other countries," he said. "Foreign governments should not be in charge of our immigration policies."

According to documents from Immigration and Customs Enforcement, 23 countries are considered largely uncooperative in taking back their citizens. The countries include China and important allies like

India and Afghanistan, as well as several African countries with close ties to the United States, among them Ghana, Liberia and Sierra Leone.

Countries often refuse to take individuals identified for deportation because of a lack of proper identification, problems in confirming citizenship, or poor record-keeping.

Zhu Haiquan, a spokesman for the Chinese Embassy in Washington, said that his government tried to work with the Department of Homeland Security in deportation cases, but that the Chinese authorities must first receive proof that the person being deported is a Chinese citizen. "We adhere to the principle of first verification, then repatriation," he said.

The Haitian Embassy in Washington did not respond to questions about the case of Mr. Jacques, the man sentenced in the Connecticut murder case.

But in communications with State Department and Homeland Security officials, the Haitian authorities said they had denied Mr. Jacques re-entry because he could not prove that he was a citizen.

Mr. Jacques arrived in the United States in 1992 after being intercepted in a boat off the Florida coast. In 1996, he was involved in a fight in Connecticut in which one man was killed and another was shot in the head but survived. Mr. Jacques was convicted of attempted murder and weapons charges. He served 15 years.

In January 2012, he was released into the custody of Immigration and Customs Enforcement and held for 205 days while officials worked to send him to Haiti. The Haitian government agreed to take him late that year, only to back out at the last minute, citing his lack of identity documents.

An investigation by the inspector general of the Department of Homeland Security found that immigration officials did not raise the case with the State Department because they did not believe that it "would intervene to encourage a foreign country to accept a violent offender like Jacques."

Mr. Jacques was released on Nov. 9, 2012. In June 2015, he fatally stabbed Ms. Chadwick in a dispute over drugs.

Migrants Confront Judgment Day Over Old Deportation Orders

BY VIVIAN YEE | MARCH 4, 2017

THERE ARE A LITTLE more than two weeks between Juan, an electrician in the Bronx, and the date he cannot forget: March 21, 2017, at 8 a.m., when the federal government has told him to report for deportation.

Two weeks to decide: Avoid it, and try to preserve the American life he has built for a little longer, even as a fugitive. Go, and lose it all: his wife and son, his job, his apartment, his world.

"I would feel like an animal if I stay here and hide," said Juan, 29, who asked that his last name not be used. "I want to prove that I can follow the laws. I want to make my case at this meeting, but I know that if I go, they're going to deport me."

In an immigration system mottled with escape hatches and hobbled by scant resources, Juan, who fled Colombia six years ago, is one of nearly a million people who have managed to linger in the United States despite having been ordered out of the country by an immigration judge — some of them more than a decade ago.

And with the Trump administration intent on sweeping perhaps millions of immigrants without legal status out of the country, the White House has not had to look far to make a quick mark. Because people with deportation orders have had their day in court, most of them can be sent out of the country without seeing a judge, sometimes within hours of being arrested.

"People who have been ordered deported and who are still here are the low-hanging fruit," said Stephen Yale-Loehr, an immigration law professor at Cornell University. "Trump has said he has wanted to deport more people. The easiest way to get those numbers up are to take those people who've been ordered deported and go after them."

President Trump's immigration agency has already offered what looks like a preview: Immigration and Customs Enforcement agents recently deported to Mexico an Arizona mother who had been ordered out of the country four years ago.

But the follow-up will be complicated. The backlog of what the government calls "fugitive aliens" has persisted through Republican and Democratic administrations, inflamed conservatives who oppose illegal immigration, and resisted the immigration authorities' attempts at enforcement.

Since 2006, even as the overall total of unauthorized immigrants in the United States has dipped, the number facing outstanding deportation orders has grown by more than half, to around 962,000 people from 632,726. More than half of them come from Mexico, El Salvador, Guatemala or Honduras. (Another 13,200 or so, as of early February, were already in the custody of customs officials.)

Despite the Bush and Obama administrations' oft-stated commitments to focus on expelling those who pose a serious danger to their communities, slightly less than one in five people facing deportation has been convicted of a crime in the United States.

The causes for delays can vary. Deportations have been deferred for humanitarian reasons — like allowing mothers to stay with sick children in the United States — or they have been frozen while an appeal is mounted. The Obama administration put off deportations for thousands of immigrants it did not consider priorities, including Juan, the Bronx electrician, and Guadalupe García de Rayos, the Arizona mother, often law-abiding people with strong ties to their communities.

"Felons, not families; criminals, not children," President Barack Obama said in 2014, describing the kinds of people he wanted deported. The government also postponed deportations for people who were likely to face torture if they were sent back.

Some deportations are simply impossible to carry out: About a quarter of the immigrants with outstanding deportation orders come from countries that refuse to take back deportees, including China, Haiti, Brazil and India.

Mr. Trump has threatened to stop issuing visas to people from these countries. In the past, diplomats have urged caution on this front, not wanting to disrupt international relationships over the issue of deportees.

And many people under final orders have slipped through gaping cracks in the immigration system. Court notices — either mailed to outdated addresses or illegible to Spanish speakers — are routinely missed, leaving judges to issue deportation orders for people who miss their chance to argue their case. Nearly a quarter of judges' decisions rendered in 2015, for example, involved cases where the immigrant in question was absent.

The months and, sometimes, years it takes for immigration and asylum cases to wind through a clogged court system can cause the authorities to lose track of immigrants living and working in the country, because they have fled or simply moved.

The White House has sought to make it harder for immigrants to be remain free inside the United States while their requests for asylum plod through the courts. They will be detained more often, or asked to wait in Mexico until a judge can rule.

"There are all kinds of things in the system that weren't built to maximize compliance," said David A. Martin, a professor of immigration law at the University of Virginia and a former immigration official in the Obama and Clinton administrations. It led to a climate, he said, that has prompted many people to not consider a deportation order a serious matter. "And that's one of the attitudes that sometimes infuriates, with some justification, people who voted for Donald Trump."

In a significant break from his predecessor, Mr. Trump is directing immigration agents to go after virtually anyone who is in the United States illegally, ending the reprieve for people who had not been considered priorities. "Ensure that aliens ordered removed from the United States are promptly removed," one line of Mr. Trump's executive order on immigration reads, with the crispness of a traffic sign.

"What has been lacking, up until a month ago, is a willingness and a commitment on the part of the administration to actually do it," said

CAITLIN O'HARA FOR THE NEW YORK TIMES

Guadalupe García de Rayos, with her son Angel, 16, was arrested in Phoenix and deported on the same day last month.

Ira Mehlman, a spokesman for the Federation for American Immigration Reform, which supports stricter immigration controls. "Nothing is easy," he said, but going after people who already have deportation orders "will be the easiest part of enforcing the president's removal priorities."

President George W. Bush's administration dented the backlog by deploying fugitive teams that were supposed to track down unauthorized immigrants with deportation orders and criminal records. But the strategy drew a backlash when the raids began snaring undocumented immigrants who were not targets.

"That was something that caused a lot of controversy and a lot of anxiety in immigrant communities, because it meant these officers could stop anyone at any time," said Randy Capps, the director of research at the Migration Policy Institute, a nonpartisan think tank. Mr. Capps added that while the Obama administration narrowed the scope of such raids, he expected the Trump administration to return to the Bush model.

There is, of course, an easier way to find some people with final orders: Wait for them to walk into ICE offices for their scheduled appointments. Ms. Rayos was driven across the border within hours of her check-in in Phoenix, and her deportation has haunted immigrants with coming appointments ever since.

But the Trump administration has yet to show a consistent hand.

Roxana Orellana Santos, 37, was allowed to walk out of her appointment in Baltimore last week. Ms. Santos, who said she had fled domestic abuse in El Salvador, was arrested in 2008 while eating lunch outdoors, her lawyers say, leading to a civil rights lawsuit that claimed she had been racially profiled. She had been ordered deported two years before that arrest, after she missed an immigration court hearing. Her lawyers said she could not read the notice, which was in English.

Ms. Santos's next appointment is in August. "I don't feel assured of what the outcome's going to be next time," she said, adding that she had asked her brother to help her husband care for her four children if she was deported.

In the case of Juan, the electrician, nothing remains to stop the government from acting on the deportation order he first received in 2013. Juan had requested asylum after paramilitary forces in Colombia tried to kill him, he said, but he lost his final appeal the month Mr. Trump was elected president.

"I feel hopeless," Juan said. "My wife is here, my son is here, they are my world. I have nowhere else to run to. I've run out of options. I don't know what to do."

Pain of Deportation Swells When Children Are Left Behind

BY ELISABETH MALKIN | MAY 20, 2017

SAN SIMÓN EL ALTO, MEXICO — When Alejandro Cedillo was deported to Mexico from the United States, his Florida-born son and daughter were little older than toddlers, and it would be six years before he would see them again. Mr. Cedillo returned, alone, to his close-knit family in San Simón el Alto, the hilltop farming town he had left nine years before, when he was only 17.

To an outsider, the gold-green fields rolling across Mexico's central plain seem to promise a chance at a decent living. But drive into places like San Simón, where the concrete houses stand incomplete and the paved road peters out, and the poverty that drives people to leave for the United States comes into focus.

Like Mr. Cedillo, now 32, many of them eventually come back. Some are deported; others return to care for a sick parent or simply decide it is time to leave the United States. But the homecoming is never the end of the story. The sequel is rarely simple, and for those with children left behind, it is agonizing.

Under President Trump's more aggressive enforcement policies, arrests of undocumented immigrants were up almost 40 percent in the first three months of his administration compared with the same period last year, and Mexico is preparing to receive a wave of returnees.

Migrant advocates here have been arguing that the newcomers need jobs, counseling and help with Mexico's cumbersome bureaucracy if they are to restart in a country that most of them left more than a decade ago.

President Enrique Peña Nieto has allocated an additional $50 million to Mexico's consulates to help migrants in the United States, and the country's Congress has changed the law to make it easier for children who have returned to enroll in school. Some state governments are offering small grants to repatriated migrants who are setting up businesses.

But when Mr. Cedillo was deported in 2010, there were no such programs to ease readjustment.

More than two million Mexicans were deported, and an unknown number crossed back on their own, during the Obama administration, and they have been trying to remake their lives since, reuniting with families changed over time and serving as cultural guides for their American-born children.

After arriving home, Mr. Cedillo found that the money he had earned up north helped soften the hardship of his childhood. He got construction work in the nearby city of Toluca, built a house and rented land with his father and brothers to grow corn and avocados.

In America, however, the family he had left behind began to unravel. His wife found a new partner, and the authorities in Florida, judging the couple unfit as parents, placed the children, Ángel and Alejandra, in foster care. When Mr. Cedillo received a registered letter asking him to waive his parental rights, he decided to fight back.

"I want them to be with me, to give them values," said Mr. Cedillo. "There are children who get everything, but they are lost, they turn to drugs."

Forbidden to enter the United States, he needed a way to persuade a family court judge in Fort Pierce, Fla., to allow him to raise his own children. There was a home for them in Mexico, but at first he found little sympathy from the court.

"It was a hard case. Everybody was against me," Mr. Cedillo said. "They said the children couldn't come here because they didn't speak Spanish, they were coming to a culture that was very different."

Desperate, he found help from the Corner Institute, which works with returning migrants in the town of Malinalco, a short drive down the mountain from San Simón. Migrants knock at the institute's wooden door with problems that reflect the complexities of families that straddle two nations.

There is the young woman with two small children, widowed when her husband died trying to cross the border. A family is seeking help after having lost touch with a daughter who left for the United States with a man the family did not trust. A wife needed assistance finding her husband, only to learn that he had been deported and was too ashamed to go home to her.

"Migrants are susceptible in these areas where there's no communication," said Ellen Calmus, the institute's director. "They are in these informational black holes when they cross the border."

These struggles affect migrants both when they are detained — and after they have returned to Mexico and need to navigate agencies in the United States, as Mr. Cedillo was forced to do to win back his children. "That's where things start going terribly wrong, and it's an invisible humanitarian crisis," Ms. Calmus said. She obtained a Florida lawyer for Mr. Cedillo, and he won the custody case. In October, the children arrived to a father they barely remembered and a country they did not know.

Mr. Cedillo is now a constant presence in his children's lives, dropping them off at school and picking them up. There, Alejandra, 9 and withdrawn, is protected by two effervescent cousins, Yaczuri and Cintia. Ángel, 10, who speaks better Spanish, has adapted more quickly.

The struggles of Mr. Cedillo's return are familiar to families across the region. Nearly everyone in San Simón, Malinalco and the nearby town of Chalma seems to know someone who has migrated to the United States. The mayor of the Malinalco municipality, Baldemar Chaqueco Reynoso, is the only one of six siblings who did not leave.

Several members of his family now have legal residency, but his younger brother Cuauhtémoc, 38, was deported three years ago, after 16 years in the United States. He and his wife, Isabel Mancilla, 37, faced a difficult decision over whether she and the couple's four children should come back with him. Their eldest daughter, Lorna, had finished her freshman year in a suburban Cleveland high school, and they were concerned about her education in Mexico.

Felipe Castañeda in San Simón el Alto, en route to the avocado grove where he works. Deported in 2008, he wants to return to the United States legally as a temporary worker.

But the whole family returned, and for Lorna, the first year was hard. She struggled with depression and fitting in at her Mexican high school. "One day I looked in the mirror and thought, 'Who am I?' " she said.

The wrenching change made Lorna, 17, a cultural observer. "There, everybody was busy with school and work, and here you have more time for family," she said. "There you have a bunch of money, but you're going to waste it going shopping."

For a region with so many migrants, there are few signs of prosperity from the dollars earned up north. Migrants send back money to pay for schooling or to build houses, said the mayor, the elder Mr. Chaqueco. "There are very few who have the discipline to save for a business," he said. Many buy taxis and rent them out to relatives. Because so many migrants have worked at carwashes in the United States, rudimentary versions have popped up along the road between Malinalco and Chalma. One of those is run by Orlando and Jaime

Arizmendi, whose seven older brothers and sisters all live legally in the United States.

Bálfre Arizmendi, 77, the men's father, first went to California in 1976 to work in the fields. In 1986, he became a legal resident and began a cycle of border crossings set by the rhythm of the seasons. "I went every year for seven months to work, and then I came back to plant here and teach the children how to work," he said. He retired in Mexico, where his American Social Security check goes further, but his children stayed in California. "Now they don't want to come back," he said.

That easy movement across the border is out of reach for many of the returned migrants who hope to work again in the United States. Felipe Castañeda, deported in 2008, cannot wait to return. He left San Simón as a young man to work in the Florida citrus groves and stayed for 15 years. With no criminal record, Mr. Castañeda applied to return to the United States as a temporary worker and was told that he would have to wait until next year, 10 years after he was deported. He is 45 now, earning about $6.50 a day overseeing 20 acres of avocado trees. The wage is not low for this area, but it cannot compare with what Mr. Castañeda could make picking crops in the United States. "My old boss told me that he needs me," Mr. Castañeda said.

Deportation a 'Death Sentence' to Adoptees After a Lifetime in the U.S.

BY CHOE SANG-HUN | **JULY 2, 2017**

SEOUL, SOUTH KOREA — Phillip Clay was adopted at 8 into an American family in Philadelphia. Twenty-nine years later, in 2012, after numerous arrests and a struggle with drug addiction, he was deported back to his birth country, South Korea. He could not speak the local language, did not know a single person and did not receive appropriate care for mental health problems, which included bipolar disorder and alcohol and substance abuse.

On May 21, Mr. Clay ended his life, jumping from the 14th floor of an apartment building north of Seoul. He was 42.

To advocates of the rights of international adoptees, the suicide was a wrenching reminder of a problem the United States urgently needed to address: adoptees from abroad who never obtained American citizenship. The Adoptee Rights Campaign, an advocacy group, estimates that 35,000 adult adoptees in the United States may lack citizenship, which was not granted automatically in the adoption process before 2000.

Mr. Clay is believed to be just one of dozens of people, legally adopted as children into American families, who either have been deported to the birth countries they left decades ago or face deportation after being convicted of crimes as adults. Some did not even know they were not American citizens until they were ordered to leave.

Adoptees from other countries, like Vietnam, Thailand and Brazil, have faced deportation. But the sheer number of children adopted from South Korea, once a leading source of children put up for adoption abroad, has made it the most visible example of the issue, and of the enormous challenges returnees face as they try to once again navigate a foreign culture, this time with little or no assistance.

Many have nowhere to go, often living on the streets. In South Korea, one deportee served a prison term for robbing a bank with a toy gun. Another, who like Mr. Clay had mental health problems, has been indicted twice on assault charges.

"Deportation is like the death sentence to them," said Hellen Ko, a chief counselor at the government-run Korea Adoption Services, who monitored Mr. Clay as a caseworker. "They had a hard time adjusting to life in America. It gets even harder for them when they return here."

The government here does not know how many of the 110,000 South Korean children adopted into American families since the 1950s have been deported. When the United States deports Koreans, it does not tell Seoul if they are adoptees. At least six cases have been documented, though, and officials here say that they have been unable to determine the citizenship status of 18,000 Korean adoptees in the United States.

Once back in their birth country, they are on their own and often go undocumented. "All I had was $20 on me; I didn't know where I was," Monte Haines said, recalling the day he landed at Seoul's gateway airport after being deported in 2009, more than 30 years after an American family adopted him. "There was nobody there to talk to."

Americans have adopted more than 350,000 children from abroad since the 1940s, according to the Adoptee Rights Campaign, and the United States left it to the parents to secure citizenship for the children.

But some did not understand that their children did not automatically become citizens when they completed the adoption. Other adoptees have said that their parents were put off by the cost and paperwork of the citizenship process, or that they essentially abandoned them.

In 2000, Congress passed the Child Citizenship Act, which granted automatic citizenship to children adopted by United States citizens. But the law did not retroactively benefit adoptees who were already legal adults.

This omission left adult adoptees with criminal records but not citizenship, like Mr. Clay and Mr. Haines, vulnerable to deportation as

America has become increasingly aggressive in pursuing illegal immigrants in recent years.

Immigration law allows the federal government to deport noncitizen immigrants found guilty of a wide range of "aggravated felonies," which include battery, forged checks and selling drugs.

Immigration and Customs Enforcement, or ICE, was unable to say how many adoptees without citizenship had been deported. The New York Times Magazine reported in 2015 that at least three dozen international adoptees had faced deportation charges or had been deported. With President Trump pledging to increase deportations, adoption advocates fear that the number will climb, with devastating consequences for those deported.

"As a child, I didn't ask to be sent to the United States. I didn't ask to learn the English language. I didn't ask to be a culturalized American," said Adam Crapser, who was deported to South Korea last year, at age 41, after 38 years in the United States. "And now I was forced back to Korea, and I lost my American family."

Mr. Crapser, who left behind a wife and three daughters in the United States, was abandoned by his first adoptive parents and abused by his second. He accumulated a criminal record over the years, including a conviction on burglary charges. But in recent years, he had begun turning his life around and applied for a green card in 2012. That triggered a background check, leading to the deportation proceedings that flipped his life upside down.

"They waited until I had a family, and they waited until I had children," he said. "They waited until I had something to lose."

Mr. Crapser, who had never traveled abroad while living in the United States, said he "could not read a sign" when he landed at Incheon Airport outside Seoul. Korean faces and the language swirling around him came as "a complete shock," he said.

His deportation put a strain on his relationship with his wife in the United States, and he has not seen his daughters in 15 months. Living out of suitcases in a tiny studio in Seoul, Mr. Crapser said that he struggled to keep himself busy to fight depression and that his job opportunities were extremely limited. "The language is the biggest barrier because of how late I came back here to Korea," he said.

Mr. Haines, another South Korea-born deportee, said he could barely pay his rent and buy food with the $5 an hour he earned as a bartender in Seoul. "I have been here for eight and a half years, and I am still having a hard time to survive," he said.

South Korea has begun devising post-adoption services in recent years, as more adoptees have returned. But returnees like Mr. Clay suffered an added obstacle in their birth country, where a cultural stigma against mental illness made it difficult for them to get proper care.

Mr. Clay, also known by his Korean name, Kim Sang-pil, was found abandoned in Seoul in 1981, according to Holt Children's Services, the adoption agency that sent him to the United States.

His first adoption into an American family in 1983 did not work out. He was placed with another family in Philadelphia a year later. Reached by email, his American father, Joseph Clay, declined to answer questions for this article.

ICE said Mr. Clay had been deported after "accumulating a lengthy criminal history dating back nearly two decades — the most serious of which included criminal convictions for robbery and multiple theft and drug-related offenses." Holt also said it had learned from Mr. Clay's American family that he had been in and out of mental hospitals.

Back in South Korea, Mr. Clay also lived his life going in and out of mental clinics and being shunted back and forth among social agencies like Holt and the Korea Adoption Services. None of them, critics said, provided him with the assistance he needed. A 2014 medical record from a South Korean hospital showed that he had been given a diagnosis of bipolar affective disorder.

In January, Mr. Clay drank paint thinner and was hospitalized. But mental clinics often did not want him because they did not have an English-speaking staff. "He said he wanted to die," said Ms. Ko, his caseworker. "He said there was nothing he could do in South Korea."

South Korea sent a delegation to the United States Congress this spring to appeal for support for the Adoptee Citizenship Act, a proposed law that would give citizenship to anyone adopted before turning 18, regardless of how long ago the adoption took place. The bill stalled in Congress during the election last year, but advocates are campaigning to reintroduce it.

After Mr. Clay's death, South Korean government officials said they were discussing better protection for deportees. But Mr. Crapser, who believes he should have automatically become a naturalized American citizen, said South Korea should "stand up to the United States and say 'no' " when it deports adoptees sent over decades ago with an understanding that they would become American citizens.

Instead, South Korea expected the returnees to "be able to act, behave, work, speak, everything like a native Korean," he said. "It's impossible."

From Offices to Disney World, Employers Brace for the Loss of an Immigrant Work Force

BY VIVIAN YEE, LIZ ROBBINS AND CAITLIN DICKERSON | JAN. 9, 2018

THEY CLEAN federal office buildings in Washington and nurse older people in Boston. They are rebuilding hurricane-wrecked Houston. The Atlanta Falcons' new stadium, plumbing and heating systems at Fannie Mae's new headquarters, the porterhouse at Peter Luger Steak House and even the Disney World experience have all depended, in small part or large, on their labor.

They are the immigrants from Haiti and Central America who have staked their livelihoods on the temporary permission they received years ago from the government to live and work in the United States. Hundreds of thousands now stand to lose that status under the Trump administration, which said on Monday that roughly 200,000 immigrants from El Salvador would have to leave by September 2019 or face deportation.

Even if they remain here illegally, they, like the young immigrants known as Dreamers whose status is also in jeopardy this winter, will lose their work permits, potentially scratching more than a million people from the legal work force in a matter of months. And the American companies that employ them will be forced to look elsewhere for labor, if they can get it at all.

"If you get rid of 26 percent of my employees, I guess I'm going to have to terminate some of the contracts," said Victor Moran, 52, the chief executive of Total Quality, a janitorial services company in the Washington area — "unless I'm willing to break the law," which he said he was not. The company employs 228 people with temporary protected status, or T.P.S., all but a handful from El Salvador.

Within the complex and often perplexing American immigration system, immigrants covered by T.P.S. fall into an especially vexed category.

Noe Duarte came to the United States from El Salvador in 2000, fleeing violence and poverty in his hometown, and was granted temporary status the following year.

The Trump administration has emphasized that the permissions were originally granted because of wars and natural disasters in the immigrants' home countries and intended to last only until conditions there improved. But in reality, their permissions have been extended so long that they have become indefinite residents, often buying homes and raising American-born children, even though their status offers no path to citizenship. They, like other unauthorized immigrants, have become indispensable parts of certain industries, taking jobs that employers say no one else will and that immigration restrictionists say could attract Americans if companies were willing to pay more.

"T.P.S. does not exist for the convenience of industries that rely on low-wage foreign labor," said Ira Mehlman, a spokesman for the Federation for American Immigration Reform.

The companies create "self-fulfilling prophecies" by offering little pay and grueling conditions, he said: "When Americans reject the wages and working conditions they offer, they then argue that Americans are unwilling to take the jobs."

Concentrated in California, Texas, Florida, New York, Virginia and Maryland, those with protected status work mainly in construction, restaurants and grocery stores, and as landscapers and day care workers, according to data on recipients from El Salvador, Honduras and Haiti assembled by the Center for Migration Studies, a nonprofit that has argued for extending the program.

More than 45,000 Haitians will have to leave by July 2019; about 57,000 Hondurans are hoping, against all indications to the contrary, that they will be spared the next time the Trump administration must decide whether to extend their protections.

Another report, by the Immigrant Legal Resource Center, estimates that stripping the protections from Salvadorans, Hondurans and Haitians would deprive Social Security and Medicare of about $6.9 billion in contributions over a decade, and would shrink the gross domestic product by $45.2 billion.

Construction companies already confronting a nationwide labor shortage will have to replace workers from what industry executives said was a minuscule pool, or turn down projects.

"There are no Americans out there to take the jobs," said Mark Drury, a vice president at Shapiro & Duncan, a Washington-area plumbing, heating and cooling firm. The company and its competitors have resorted to poaching each other's project managers, engineers, welders and plumbers.

The company even retrained and hired a former coal miner who decided to switch careers, Mr. Drury said, but had not found other miners willing to move to the area.

Not only will the company have to lay off its 14 Salvadoran workers, Mr. Drury said, but it was also worrying about the roughly 30 employees who are protected from deportation by virtue of a government program for immigrants who were brought to the country illegally as children. The Trump administration has announced that the program, Deferred Action for Childhood Arrivals, will expire in March.

Congress is considering creating a new program for those immigrants, perhaps in exchange for new border security spending, but no deal has been reached. On Tuesday, President Trump said he was open to a comprehensive deal that would shield not only the young immigrants, but perhaps millions of others without legal status, presumably including those with temporary protected status.

That would be a welcome development to Mr. Drury, who said he had about 40 openings. The company — which is helping to build a cancer center, the new headquarters of the mortgage giant Fannie Mae and a project at the headquarters of the National Security Agency — was already turning away work because it could not hire fast enough, he said. "Losing people just puts us further behind," he said.

For Stan Marek, the chief executive of Marek, a Houston-based construction company, the decisions to end temporary protections have come at the worst possible time. Houston is waiting to be rebuilt after Hurricane Harvey, yet, he said, there will be fewer people than ever to overhaul the city's office buildings, schools, hotels and hospitals.

About 30 employees from Honduras, Haiti and El Salvador with temporary protected status have worked for him for over a decade. Some are skilled craftsmen; some are supervisors.

Mr. Marek has pushed on his workers' behalf, even paying for a public-relations campaign to call for immigration reform.

"If they lose their status — boom, we'll have to terminate them, and that's not much fun, telling a guy who's got three kids in high school, all American-born, that he's going to be terminated," Mr. Marek said. "They're good people, damn good people."

Though they will be subject to deportation, many immigrants who lose their temporary protections are likely to stay in the United States.

Asked what he planned to do when his status expired next year, Noe Duarte said he and his wife and two adult children, who are already living here illegally, would simply "hide."

Mr. Duarte came to the United States from El Salvador in 2000, fleeing violence and poverty in his hometown, and was granted temporary status the following year. His family operates two small companies, cleaning and painting houses, in Gaithersburg, Md. When business is slow, Mr. Duarte works as a safety supervisor for a major construction company.

Even knowing that their finances would crater without his work permit, he felt that the family would be safer here than in El Salvador. "The country is infested with gangs," he said. "The moment we arrived, they would come to our door asking for money. And if we didn't give it to them, we'd be killed."

Mr. Moran, the janitorial services executive, had been worried about the impending cancellation of the program. His staff cleans buildings throughout the Washington area, including the headquarters of Immigration and Customs Enforcement, the federal agency that would be responsible for deporting his workers, and the offices of the special prosecutor, Robert S. Mueller III.

A Trump voter who said he supported the president's overall approach to immigration, Mr. Moran refuses to hire unauthorized immigrants, saying he believes such hiring practices leave those workers more vulnerable to wage abuse and poor treatment. (And, if caught, his firm could also face prosecution and large fines.) Mr. Moran, himself an immigrant from Spain, hopes that immigration reform will eventually happen under Mr. Trump. Until then, he said, "it could be painful" for thousands of people to uproot their lives.

It will not be easy on employers, either. Assisted living facilities that rely on skilled nurses to care for older and sick people already struggle to attract applicants to jobs that are both physically and emotionally taxing, said Christopher Donnellan, the director of government relations for the American Healthcare Association, an assisted living facility trade group. His affiliates were already shaken once, in November, when the Trump administration announced it would rescind protected status for Haitians, who make up a majority of the staff in some facilities in the Boston area. Salvadorans with protected status make up an even larger proportion of the members' work force, he said.

Before the November decision, the Walt Disney Company announced that it, too, supported an extension: It said Disney World employed more than 500 protected Haitians.

Seventeen years ago, Hugo Rodriguez, 43, started as a dishwasher at the Great Neck, N.Y., an outpost of the fabled Peter Luger Steak House. Now he is a cook. Several of his co-workers also have temporary protections, he said. Receiving his permit "was the beginning of the American dream," he recalled. Now, he fears losing it will be the end.

"I can't stay illegally, I can't do it," Mr. Rodriguez said. "But that means to go back and start at the bottom."

When Migrants Are Treated Like Slaves

OPINION | BY JACQUELINE STEVENS | APRIL 4, 2018

WE'RE FAMILIAR with grim stories about black-shirted federal agents barging into apartment complexes, convenience stores and school pickup sites to round up and deport immigrants. We've heard far less about the forced labor — some call it slavery — inside detention facilities. But new legal challenges to these practices are succeeding and may stymie the government's deportation agenda by taking profits out of the detention business.

Yes, detention is a business. In 2010, private prisons and their lenders and investors lobbied Congress to pass a law ordering Immigration and Customs Enforcement to maintain contracts for no fewer than 34,000 beds per night.

This means that when detention counts are low, people who would otherwise be released because they pose no danger or flight risk and

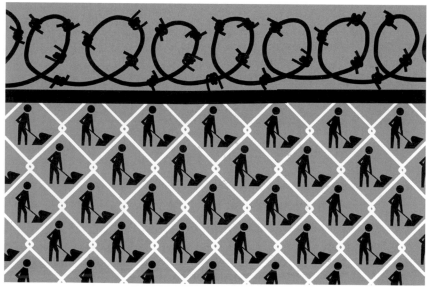

JUSTIN RENTERIA

are likely to win their cases in immigration court remain locked up, at a cost to the government of about $125 a day.

The people detained at these facilities do almost all of the work that keeps them running, outside of guard duty. That includes cooking, serving and cleaning up food, janitorial services, laundry, haircutting, painting, floor buffing and even vehicle maintenance. Most jobs pay $1 a day; some work they are required to do pays nothing.

Workers in immigration custody have suffered injuries and even died. In 2007, Cesar Gonzalez was killed in a facility in Los Angeles County when his jackhammer hit an electrical cable, sending 10,000 volts of direct current through his body. He was on a crew digging holes for posts to extend the camp's perimeter.

Crucially, California's Division of Occupational Safety and Health ruled that regardless of his status as a detainee, Mr. Gonzalez was also an employee, and his employer was found to have violated state laws on occupational safety and health.

Two of the country's biggest detention companies — GEO and CoreCivic, known as CCA — are now under attack by five lawsuits. They allege that the obligatory work and eight-hour shifts for no or little pay are unlawful. They also accuse the companies of violating state minimum wage laws, the Trafficking Victims Protection Act and laws prohibiting unjust enrichment.

The plaintiffs have a strong case. Forced labor is constitutional so long as it is a condition of punishment, a carve-out in the slavery prohibitions of the 13th Amendment. But in 1896, the Supreme Court held that "the order of deportation is not a punishment for crime." Thus, while private prisons may require work to "punish" or "correct" criminal inmates, judges in three cases have ruled that immigration detention facilities may not. It's as legal for GEO to force its facilities' residents to work as it would be to make seniors in government-funded nursing homes scrub their neighbors' showers.

GEO's own defense provides insights into just how much its profits depend on labor coerced from the people it locks up. In 2017, after

Federal District Judge John Kane certified a class-action lawsuit on behalf of GEO residents in Aurora, Colo., the company filed an appeal claiming the suit "poses a potentially catastrophic risk to GEO's ability to honor its contracts with the federal government."

Court records suggest that GEO may be paying just 1.25 percent to 6 percent of minimum wage, and as little as half of 1 percent of what federal contractors are supposed to pay under the Service Contract Act. If the plaintiffs win, that's tens of millions of dollars GEO would be obligated to pay in back wages to up to 62,000 people, not to mention additional payments going forward. And that's just at one facility.

GEO's appeal tanked. During oral arguments last summer, the company's lawyer defended the work program by explaining that those held in Aurora "make a decision each time whether they're going to consent to work or not." A judge interjected, "Or eat, or be put in isolation, right? I mean, slaves had a choice, right?" The 10th Circuit panel in February unanimously ruled that the case could proceed.

On top of that, last year GEO was sued for labor violations in its Tacoma, Wash., facility. In October, United States District Judge Robert Bryan, a Reagan appointee (!), denied GEO's motions to dismiss these cases and for the first time allowed claims under the state minimum wage laws to proceed, as well as those for forced labor and unjust enrichment.

On March 7, 18 Republican members of the House, 12 of whom have private prisons in or adjacent to their districts, sent a letter to the leaders of the departments of Labor, Justice and Homeland Security complaining about the lawsuits. They warned that if the agencies don't intervene to protect the companies, "immigration enforcement efforts will be thwarted."

Those who cheer this outcome should feel encouraged. The measures the representatives asked for — including a statement by the government that those who work while locked up are "not employees" and that federal minimum wage laws do not apply to them — won't stop the litigation. Agency pronouncements cannot overturn statutes.

As long as judges follow the laws, more of the true costs of deportation will be put into the ledgers.

If the price of human suffering does not deter the barbarism of rounding people up based on the happenstance of birth, then maybe pinched taxpayer wallets will.

JACQUELINE STEVENS is a professor of political science and runs the Deportation Research Clinic at Northwestern University.

Deported, and Sticking Out: 'This Ain't Home. America's My Home.'

BY HANNAH BEECH | MARCH 11, 2018

PHNOM PENH, CAMBODIA — It was fish for breakfast and fish for lunch and fish for dinner.

"I hate fish," Khan Hin said.

What Mr. Hin wanted was a burger. Maybe a bowl of Cap'n Crunch. Or some Tater Tots. "I'm feisty," he said, "for my Flamin' Hot Cheetos."

Mr. Hin's palate is American. His vernacular, slang from the streets of Stockton, Calif., is American.

And his family's experience is all too American. His older sister was at school in Stockton in 1989 when a man sprayed gunfire on the schoolyard. Five children ages 6 to 9, all of Cambodian or Vietnamese heritage, were killed. Nearly 30 others, including Mr. Hin's sister, were injured. The killer had repeatedly spewed hatred of Asian immigrants.

At the hospital, Mr. Hin's sister got to meet Michael Jackson, which was an American dream of sorts, although it wasn't worth two bullets in her body.

But Mr. Hin, 33, isn't American. Born in a Thai refugee camp, he came to the United States as a baby. His parents, refugees fleeing genocide in Cambodia, never claimed citizenship for their son, even though he was entitled to it. Until he was jailed at age 18 for auto theft, Mr. Hin had no idea he was only a legal permanent resident.

American law is uncompromising: Deportation applies to legal permanent residents who commit an aggravated felony in the United States. Such crimes include failing to appear in court or filing a false tax return, as well as more serious offenses. Deportees are barred from returning to the United States.

Mr. Hin had served five years and was holding down a job in California when Immigration and Customs Enforcement came for him. For 18 months, he shuffled through various detention centers across the United

States. Three years ago, he was deported to Cambodia. It was his first time in the country. He did not speak Khmer, the local language.

That's how Mr. Hin ended up on the outskirts of Phnom Penh, the Cambodian capital, in the house of a family friend he couldn't understand, eating fish three meals a day. "It was rats, pigs, babies all over the place," he said. "It was the ghetto but badder. This ain't home. America's my home."

While President Trump has brought renewed attention to the fate of legal and illegal immigrants alike, deportations of Cambodians began in 2002, when the government of Cambodia signed a repatriation agreement with the Bush administration. So far, around 600 legal permanent residents of Cambodian descent have been deported from the United States, many directly from prison.

The number is likely to increase significantly this year, as Mr. Trump cracks down on green card holders with criminal records. Immigration and Customs Enforcement tracks 1,900 Cambodians who are subject to orders of removal from the United States.

The Khmer Vulnerability Aid Organization, which receives American funding to help deportees start new lives in Cambodia, expects around 200 people to arrive this year. Around 100 Cambodians who had already completed their prison terms were rounded up in immigration raids in October.

Citing human rights concerns, the Cambodian government suspended the repatriation agreement last year. But the United States responded by slapping visa restrictions on Cambodian officials, and a trickle of deportations began in December. In February, the two governments held talks on the repatriations, and 16 deportees have arrived this year.

Posy Chheng was deported last May, just a couple weeks after his son was born. His wife grew up in Minnesota farm country and knew nothing about the American secret bombing campaign in Cambodia or the ensuing reign of terror unleashed by the Khmer Rouge. At least 1.7 million Cambodians died by execution, disease or starvation when the Communist guerrilla movement took over in the late 1970s.

"Goulash and spaghetti," Mr. Chheng said of his wife. "That's her life." When he was 14 years old, Mr. Chheng was convicted as an adult of second-degree murder and imprisoned for 17 years. After his release five years ago, he worked as a barber in St. Paul and spent time with his mother, who had raised four children on her own. His own son is still in Minnesota.

"I think about him all the time," Mr. Chheng said. "I see kids without car seats here, squeezed on a motorcycle with their whole family, and I think: 'No way I'd let my son do that. It's crazy.' "

Asian immigrants are often regarded as a model minority group in the United States, with higher education and income levels than other ethnic groups. But the 270,000 people of Cambodian descent who live in the United States are among the poorest in the country.

Many Cambodian refugees were farmers who fled the Khmer Rouge with no schooling or savings. Once in the United States, they scrambled to get menial jobs, like packing fruit or sewing clothes.

ADAM DEAN FOR THE NEW YORK TIMES

Ricky Kul, rear, became a gang member in Los Angeles out of self-defense, he says. Unlike many deportees to Cambodia, he feels grateful. "If I wasn't here, I might be dead," he said.

"My mom was illiterate, she didn't speak any English," said Jimmy Hiem, who was deported to Cambodia in 2016. "I'd get up to go to school, and she'd be sewing. I'd go to bed, and she'd be sewing. How was she supposed to know anything about citizenship and stuff like that?"

Cambodian refugees, along with Vietnamese and Laotians, were often resettled in tough neighborhoods, like South Central Los Angeles or Long Beach. By the 1980s, their children had formed street gangs, like the notorious Tiny Rascal Gang.

"We had to protect ourselves from homeboy shootouts," said Ricky Kul, who was 15 when he joined the Oriental Lazy Boyz in Los Angeles and was later jailed for burglary. (Three members of the Oriental Lazy Boyz were convicted of the 1996 murder of Haing Ngor, the Cambodian-American actor who won an Academy Award for his role in "The Killing Fields.")

Mr. Kul, who was repatriated two years ago, now manages a bar in Phnom Penh that is popular with foreign visitors. If deportees lack

ADAM DEAN FOR THE NEW YORK TIMES

Posy Chheng, 36, was a barber back in Minnesota before being deported to Phnom Penh last year. His year-old son and wife are still back in the States.

the tattoos that mark them as gangbangers, they can find work as English teachers or tour guides. One runs a hip-hop dance academy, another is a street poet.

While some deportees have taken their own lives or been caught dealing drugs, the recidivism rate in Cambodia is lower than in the United States, according to Bill Herod, the founder of the Khmer Vulnerability Aid Organization.

"If I wasn't here, I might be dead," Mr. Kul, 42, said. "Leaving America kind of forced me to turn my life around."

The one thing he misses, though, is his mother, who has diabetes. She did whatever she could to support the family, like digging oysters or sorting through recycling. "She had a rough life, always hustling for her kids," Mr. Kul said.

Modern Phnom Penh, with its Domino's Pizza outlets and air-conditioned malls, would be unimaginable for his mother, he admitted. Her memories of home are of bombs and piles of dead bodies higher than any rice harvest.

"I'm going to get myself on my feet," Mr. Kul said, "and then I'm going to bring her here and show her, 'Look at my life, look at Cambodia.' She can finally be proud."

Deporting the American Dream

OPINION | BY ANITA ISAACS AND ANNE PRESTON | JULY 9, 2018

Ms. Isaacs is a political scientist who specializes in Central and Latin America. Ms. Preston is an economist.

MEXICO CITY — To hear the Trump administration talk about the immigrants it has deported back to Mexico, you would think they were all criminals and potential drains on the nation's economy and welfare system, with no interest in participating in what used to be called the American dream.

In fact, none of that is true. We know, because the two of us talked to hundreds of them.

Over the last few weeks we were in Mexico, beginning an oral history project documenting the migrant experience. Over the course of three weeks our team surveyed and interviewed more than 200 returning Mexican migrants, the vast majority of them deportees. Some were caught in roadblocks. Others were pulled over for running a stop light or for speeding. They were detained in American county jails and immigration detention centers before being sent to Mexico. Many had lived in the United States almost their entire lives.

And yet, despite that experience, when we asked them what they missed about the United States, their responses were automatic: "everything." "I feel American," they told us over and over again. And why wouldn't they? They grew up as the kids next door. They went to our children's schools and birthday parties. They attended our churches, played on our sports teams. As high schoolers they flipped hamburgers at McDonald's.

But they also always had it a little rougher. Occasionally they faced discrimination. Their parents worked multiple jobs, often seven days a week. They left home before their children woke up and returned long after they were asleep. Children as young as 8 shouldered the burdens of caring for younger siblings. They began working as soon as they reached high school. But their unauthorized status limited their job opportunities; they couldn't get a driver's license and college was a remote possibility. Some got into the same kind of trouble native-born children do, but most worked hard to keep their families afloat.

Still, the American dream meant everything to them. In optimistic terms rarely heard from native-born Americans, they described the United States as a place where success was possible. Whether they lived in a big city or small town, in a red state or a blue state, they overwhelmingly recall an American society that was genuine, open, diverse and accepting.

One man teared up remembering his childhood friend, Matthew, with whom he played baseball, swam in the neighborhood pool and shared tacos and mac and cheese. Another missed ice fishing on frozen Minnesota lakes, using snowmobiles fashioned with special drills that he helped assemble through his work at a fiberglass factory. He shared another memory: After introducing his friends to guacamole, they insisted on eating at his place. "We had an arrangement: They'd bring the avocados," he'd make the dip.

A young woman recalled being terrified of having her friends discover her unauthorized status. When she finally found the courage to tell them, they reassured her that they couldn't care less, and laughingly nicknamed her the "alien."

Each deportee stressed the kindness of ordinary Americans who lent a helping hand. Bosses who gave them a chance, appreciated their hard work, mentored their success. Teachers whose names are etched in their memories: Mr. McDonald, Mrs. Wilson, Miss Annie — all went the extra mile to help them succeed in school. Coaches made it possible for them to play on club soccer or mighty mites football teams by paying their dues and buying them the uniforms their parents couldn't afford. A young man cried, remembering the marine who helped him find his way as a troubled adolescent.

Back in Mexico, these returning migrants are desperately strug-gling to find their place in a foreign country. One young woman return-ing from Fort Myers, Fla., said, "I didn't even know what Mexican earth was like and whether the sun shone."

The returnees stand out. They dress differently, they think differ-ently, they speak broken Spanish and they dream in English. They miss everyday American life and its special occasions. They long for American food, rattling off every conceivable American chain restau-rant. Several insist that Mexican tacos couldn't begin to compete with Taco Bell. They are American football fans rather than soccer aficio-nados. A handful confess they aren't following the World Cup because the United States didn't qualify.

They can still proudly recite the Pledge of Allegiance and sing the United States national anthem. They loved observing United States holidays and several still do even back in Mexico. On Thanksgiving they expressed gratitude for opportunities the United States provided them. On July 4, they celebrated a country where "everyone praises each other's successes."

They reminisce about living in a country governed by the rule of law. Our survey asks them whether they were fearful of United States authorities. Except for the newest deportees who experienced the recent crackdowns, respondents react with a quizzical look, followed by an almost universal "no." They surprise themselves with their answers, because as undocumented migrants they had every reason to be fear-ful. Yet the vast majority contrast the crime, corruption and lawless-ness that pervades Mexico with the safety they felt in the United States, a place they describe as one "where police can't be bribed," "where peo-ple obey rules" and "where kids can play safely outside."

Separated from their families and friends, many live immersed in childhood memories. Others, like Israel Concha, the director of New Comienzos, an organization of returning migrants with which we col-laborated, have become activists committed to bringing the American dream to Mexico. They enact practices and values they acquired in the United States, notably volunteerism, a custom foreign to many Mexicans but "something we all learned to do in the United States," Mr. Concha explains.

We watched these volunteer workers reach out to the scores of returning Mexican migrants who pass through their doors every day. They are always welcoming and upbeat. They encourage those who feel isolated to join their team. They link those who suffer depression with counseling centers. They provide clothing to the destitute, accompany battered women to shelters and help returning migrants find job training and work opportunities.

These memories of migrant life in the United States stand in stark contrast to the inhumane crackdown simultaneously unfolding at the border. The returning migrants we met are products of an American society that is forgetting its identity. In a cruel irony, organizations like New Comienzos are importing to Mexico the American values of mutual respect, open-mindedness and generosity their volunteers were raised with. Meanwhile, American children are growing up in a society where aggression, prejudice and turning a blind eye to human suffering are increasingly condoned.

ANITA ISAACS is a professor of political science at Haverford College and a global fellow at the Woodrow Wilson Center. ANNE PRESTON is a professor of economics at Haverford.

Glossary

adjudicate The act of judging a case, competition or argument, or of making a formal decision about something.

assimilate To become a part of a group, country or society.

asylum Protection given by a government to someone who has left another country in order to escape being harmed.

collateral Something pledged as security for repayment of a loan.

derogatory A term for something that is belittling.

deterrence The act of discouraging actions, particularly criminal actions, by instilling fear or doubt.

directive An official or authoritative instruction or command.

forum A meeting or internet site where ideas on a particular issue can be exchanged.

Immigration and Customs Enforcement (ICE) The federal law enforcement agency tasked with enforcing U.S. immigration policy.

migrant A person who moves from place to place to find work or better living conditions.

repercussion The unintended consequence, usually unpleasant, or an event or action.

tantamount Being almost the same or having the same effect as something, usually bad.

undocumented Someone who lives in the United States without legal immigration status.

Media Literacy Terms

"Media literacy" refers to the ability to access, understand, critically assess and create media. The following terms are important components of media literacy, and they will help you critically engage with the articles in this title.

angle The aspect of a news story that a journalist focuses on and develops.

attribution The method by which a source is identified or by which facts and information are assigned to the person who provided them.

balance Principle of journalism that both perspectives of an argument should be presented in a fair way.

byline Name of the writer, usually placed between the headline and the story.

caption Identifying copy for a picture; also called a legend or cutline.

commentary A type of story that is an expression of opinion on recent events by a journalist generally known as a commentator.

editorial Article of opinion or interpretation.

fake news A fictional or made-up story presented in the style of a legitimate news story, intended to deceive readers; also commonly used to criticize legitimate news that one dislikes because of its perspective or unfavorable coverage of a subject.

feature story Article designed to entertain as well as to inform.

headline Type, usually 18 point or larger, used to introduce a story.

human interest story A type of story that focuses on individuals and how events or issues affect their life, generally offering a sense of relatability to the reader.

impartiality Principle of journalism that a story should not reflect a journalist's bias and should contain balance.

intention The motive or reason behind something, such as the publication of a news story.

interview story A type of story in which the facts are gathered primarily by interviewing another person or persons.

motive The reason behind something, such as the publication of a news story or a source's perspective on an issue.

news story An article or style of expository writing that reports news, generally in a straightforward fashion and without editorial comment.

op-ed An opinion piece that reflects a prominent individual's opinion on a topic of interest.

paraphrase The summary of an individual's words, with attribution, rather than a direct quotation of their exact words.

quotation The use of an individual's exact words indicated by the use of quotation marks and proper attribution.

reliability The quality of being dependable and accurate, said of a journalistic source.

rhetorical device Technique in writing intending to persuade the reader or communicate a message from a certain perspective.

source The origin of the information reported in journalism.

style A distinctive use of language in writing or speech; also a news or publishing organization's rules for consistent use of language with regards to spelling, punctuation, typography and capitalization, usually regimented by a house style guide.

tone A manner of expression in writing or speech.

Media Literacy Questions

1. Compare the headlines of "Trump Moves to End DACA and Calls on Congress to Act" (on page 134) and "Deportation a 'Death Sentence' to Adoptees After a Lifetime in the U.S." (on page 189). Which is a more compelling headline, and why? How could the less compelling headline be changed to better draw the reader's interest?

2. What type of story is "Pain of Deportation Swells When Children Are Left Behind" (on page 184)? Can you identify another article in this collection that is the same type of story?

3. Does Sharon Otterman demonstrate the journalistic principle of impartiality in her article "Manhattan Church Shields Guatemalan Woman From Deportation" (on page 117)? If so, how did she do so? If not, what could she have included to make her article more impartial?

4. The article "Only Mass Deportation Can Save America" (on page 50) is an example of an op-ed. Identify how Bret Stephens's attitude, tone and point of view help convey his opinion on the topic.

5. "When Migrants Are Treated Like Slaves" (on page 200) features an illustration. What does this illustration add to the article?

6. What is the intention of the article "Is It Possible to Resist Deportation in Trump's America" (on page 90)? How effectively does it achieve its intended purpose?

7. Identify the various sources cited in the article "ICE Deportation Cases: Your Questions Answered" (on page 74). How do the journalists attribute information to each of these sources in their article? How effective are their attributions in helping the reader identify their sources?

8. In "A Twitter Rant That Rails and Misleads on Immigration Policy" (on page 39), Linda Qiu directly quotes tweets from President Trump. What are the strengths of the use of a direct quote as opposed to paraphrasing? What are the weaknesses?

9. Identify each of the sources in "Nations Hinder U.S. Effort to Deport Immigrants Convicted of Crime" (on page 175) as a primary source or a secondary source. Evaluate the reliability and credibility of each source. How does your evaluation of each source change your perspective on this article?

10. Analyze the authors' reporting in "Hundreds of Immigrant Children Have Been Taken From Parents at U.S. Border" (on page 152) and "Did the Trump Administration Separate Immigrant Children From Parents and Lose Them?" (on page 162). Do you think one journalist is more impartial in their reporting than the other? If so, why do you think so?

11. Does "Pain of Deportation Swells When Children Are Left Behind" (on page 184) use multiple sources? What are the strengths of using multiple sources in a journalistic piece? What are the weaknesses of relying heavily on one source or a few sources?

12. What is the intention of the article "From Offices to Disney World, Employers Brace for the Loss of an Immigrant Work Force" (on page 194)? How effectively does it achieve its intended purpose?

Citations

All citations in this list are formatted according to the Modern Language Association's (MLA) style guide.

BOOK CITATION

NEW YORK TIMES EDITORIAL STAFF, THE. *Deportation: Who Goes and Who Stays?* New York: New York Times Educational Publishing, 2019.

ONLINE ARTICLE CITATIONS

BAKER, PETER. "Trump Supports Plan to Cut Legal Immigration by Half." *The New York Times*, 4 Aug. 2017, https://www.nytimes.com/2017/08/02/us/politics/trump-immigration.html.

BEECH, HANNAH. "Deported, and Sticking Out: 'This Ain't Home. America's My Home.'" *The New York Times*, 11 Mar. 2018, https://www.nytimes.com/2018/03/11/world/asia/cambodia-deportees-trump.html.

BENNER, KATIE. "Justice Dept. Restricts a Common Tactic of Immigration Judges." *The New York Times*, 17 May 2018, https://www.nytimes.com/2018/05/17/us/politics/sessions-immigration-judges.html.

BORJAS, GEORGE J. "Trump Sets Up a Grand Bargain on Immigration." *The New York Times*, 2 Feb. 2018, https://www.nytimes.com/2018/02/02/opinion/trump-immigration-dreamers.html.

CHO, NIRAJ, AND VIVIAN YEE. "ICE Deportation Cases: Your Questions Answered." *The New York Times*, 13 Feb. 2018, https://www.nytimes.com/2018/02/13/us/immigration-deportation-ice.html.

DICKERSON, CAITLIN. "Hundreds of Immigrant Children Have Been Taken From Parents at U.S. Border." *The New York Times,* 20 Apr. 2018, https://www.nytimes.com/2018/04/20/us/immigrant-children-separation-ice.html.

GONZALEZ, DAVID. "Being Deported From Home for the Holidays." *The New York Times*, 26 Nov. 2017, https://www.nytimes.com/2017/11/26/nyregion/being-deported-from-home-for-the-holidays.html.

GREEN, ERICA L. "For Immigrant Students, a New Worry: A Call to ICE." *The*

New York Times, 30 May 2018, https://www.nytimes.com/2018/05/30/us/politics/immigrant-students-deportation.html.

HARMON, AMY. "Did the Trump Administration Separate Immigrant Children From Parents and Lose Them?" *The New York Times*, 28 May 2018, https://www.nytimes.com/2018/05/28/us/trump-immigrant-children-lost.html.

ISAACS, ANITA, AND ANNE PRESTON. "Deporting the American Dream." *The New York Times*, 9 Jul. 2018, https://www.nytimes.com/2018/07/09/opinion/mexico-migrants-deportation.html.

JORDAN, MIRIAM. "Is America a 'Nation of Immigrants'? Immigration Agency Says No." *The New York Times*, 22 Feb. 2018, https://www.nytimes.com/2018/02/22/us/uscis-nation-of-immigrants.html.

JORDAN, MIRIAM. "Judge Upholds Order for Trump Administration to Restore DACA." *The New York Times*, 3 Aug. 2018, https://www.nytimes.com/2018/08/03/us/federal-judge-daca.html.

JORDAN, MIRIAM. "Migrant Families Have Been Reunited. Now, a Scramble to Prevent Deportations." *The New York Times*, 30 Jul. 2018, https://www.nytimes.com/2018/07/30/us/migrant-families-deportations.html.

JORDAN, MIRIAM, AND CAITLIN DICKERSON. "More Than 450 Migrant Parents May Have Been Deported Without Their Children." *The New York Times*, 24 Jul. 2018, https://www.nytimes.com/2018/07/24/us/migrant-parents-deported-children.html.

JORDAN, MIRIAM, AND RON NIXON. "Trump Administration Threatens Jail and Separating Children From Parents for Those Who Illegally Cross Southwest Border." *The New York Times*, 7 May 2018, https://www.nytimes.com/2018/05/07/us/politics/homeland-security-prosecute-undocumented-immigrants.html.

KAPLAN, THOMAS. "What to Expect as the House Heads Toward an Immigration Showdown." *The New York Times*, 6 June 2018, https://www.nytimes.com/2018/06/06/us/politics/house-republicans-immigration.html.

MALKIN, ELISABETH. "Pain of Deportation Swells When Children Are Left Behind." *The New York Times*, 20 May 2017, https://www.nytimes.com/2017/05/20/world/americas/mexico-migrants-immigration-homecoming.html.

MAZZEI, PATRICIA. "Immigration Agents Target 7-Eleven Stores in Push to Punish Employers." *The New York Times*, 10 Jan. 2018, https://www.nytimes.com/2018/01/10/us/7-eleven-raids-ice.html.

NIXON, RON. "About 2,500 Nicaraguans to Lose Special Permission to Live in U.S." *The New York Times*, 6 Nov. 2017, https://www.nytimes.com/2017

/11/06/us/politics/immigrants-temporary-protected-status-central
-americans-haitians.html.

NIXON, RON. "Nations Hinder U.S. Effort to Deport Immigrants Convicted of
Crime." *The New York Times*, 1 Jul. 2016, https://www.nytimes.com/2016
/07/02/us/homeland-security-immigrants-criminal-conviction.html.

NIXON, RON, AND EILEEN SULLIVAN. "White House Pressed Unsuccessfully to
End Immigration Program." *The New York Times*, 9 Nov. 2017, https://www
.nytimes.com/2017/11/09/us/politics/kelly-duke-immigration-protection
-honduras.html.

OTTERMAN, SHARON. "Manhattan Church Shields Guatemalan Woman From
Deportation." *The New York Times*, 28 Mar. 2018, https://www.nytimes
.com/2018/03/28/nyregion/guatemala-deportation-church-sanctuary.html.

PARLAPIANO, ALICIA. "Dreamers' Fate Is Now Tied to Border Wall and Other
G.O.P. Immigration Demands." *The New York Times*, 15 Feb. 2018, https://
www.nytimes.com/interactive/2018/02/15/us/politics/immigration-issues
-congress-daca.html.

QIU, LINDA. "A Twitter Rant That Rails and Misleads on Immigration Policy."
The New York Times, 3 Apr. 2018, https://www.nytimes.com/2018/04/03/us
/politics/fact-check-trump-twitter-immigration-policy-.html.

ROBBINS, LIZ. "A Game of Cat and Mouse With High Stakes: Deportation." *The
New York Times*, 3 Aug. 2017, https://www.nytimes.com/2017/08/03
/nyregion/a-game-of-cat-and-mouse-with-high-stakes-deportation.html.

ROBBINS, LIZ. "Immigrants Claim Lawyers Defrauded Them and They May Be
Deported." *The New York Times*, 3 May 2018, https://www.nytimes.com
/2018/05/03/nyregion/immigrants-lawyers-defrauded-deportation.html.

ROBBINS, LIZ. "In a 'Sanctuary City,' Immigrants Are Still at Risk." *The New
York Times*, 27 Feb. 2018, https://www.nytimes.com/2018/02/27/nyregion
/sanctuary-cities-immigrants-ice.html.

SANG-HUN, CHOE. "Deportation a 'Death Sentence' to Adoptees After a Lifetime
in the U.S." *The New York Times*, 2 Jul. 2017, https://www.nytimes.com
/2017/07/02/world/asia/south-korea-adoptions-phillip-clay-adam-crapser
.html.

SANTOS, FERNANDA. "The Road, or Flight, From Detention to Deportation."
The New York Times, 20 Feb. 2017, https://www.nytimes.com/2017/02/20
/us/the-road-or-flight-from-detention-to-deportation.html.

SHEAR, MICHAEL D., AND JULIE HIRSCHFELD DAVIS. "Stoking Fears, Trump
Defied Bureaucracy to Advance Immigration Agenda." *The New York Times*,

23 Dec. 2017, https://www.nytimes.com/2017/12/23/us/politics
/trump-immigration.html.

SHEAR, MICHAEL D., AND JULIE HIRSCHFELD DAVIS. "Trump Moves to End DACA and
Calls on Congress to Act." *The New York Times*, 5 Sept. 2017, https://www
.nytimes.com/2017/09/05/us/politics/trump-daca-dreamers-immigration
.html.

SHEAR, MICHAEL D., AND RON NIXON. "New Trump Deportation Rules Allow
Far More Expulsions." *The New York Times*, 21 Feb. 2017, https://www
.nytimes.com/2017/02/21/us/politics/dhs-immigration-trump.html.

STEPHENS, BRET. "Only Mass Deportation Can Save America." *The New York
Times*, 16 Jun. 2017, https://www.nytimes.com/2017/06/16/opinion
/only-mass-deportation-can-save-america.html.

STEVENS, JACQUELINE. "When Migrants Are Treated Like Slaves." *The New
York Times*, 4 Apr. 2018, https://www.nytimes.com/2018/04/04/opinion
/migrants-detention-forced-labor.html.

VALDES, MARCELA. "Is It Possible to Resist Deportation in Trump's America?"
The New York Times, https://www.nytimes.com/2017/05/23/magazine
/is-it-possible-to-resist-deportation-in-trumps-america.html.

VILLAVICENCIO, KARLA CORNEJO. "The Americans Left Behind by Deportation."
The New York Times, 28 Feb. 2018, https://www.nytimes.com
/2018/02/28/opinion/american-families-immigrants-deportation.html.

YEE, VIVIAN. "A Marriage Used to Prevent Deportation. Not Anymore." *The
New York Times*, 19 Apr. 2018, https://www.nytimes.com/2018/04/19/us
/immigration-marriage-green-card.html.

YEE, VIVIAN. "Migrants Confront Judgment Day Over Old Deportation
Orders." *The New York Times*, 4 Mar. 2017, https://www.nytimes.com/2017
/03/04/us/migrants-facing-old-deportation-orders.html.

YEE, VIVIAN. "Prosecutors' Dilemma: Will Conviction Lead to 'Life Sentence of
Deportation'?" *The New York Times*, 31 Jul. 2017, https://www.nytimes
.com/2017/07/31/us/prosecutors-dilemma-will-conviction-lead-to-life
-sentence-of-deportation.html.

YEE, VIVIAN, ET AL. "From Offices to Disney World, Employers Brace for
the Loss of an Immigrant Work Force." *The New York Times*, 9 Jan. 2018,
https://www.nytimes.com/2018/01/09/us/immigrant-work-force
-salvadorans-haitians.html.

Index

This book is current up until the time of printing. For the most up-to-date reporting, visit www.nytimes.com.